AF597890

PALM SPRINGS 1960 • Robert Doisneau

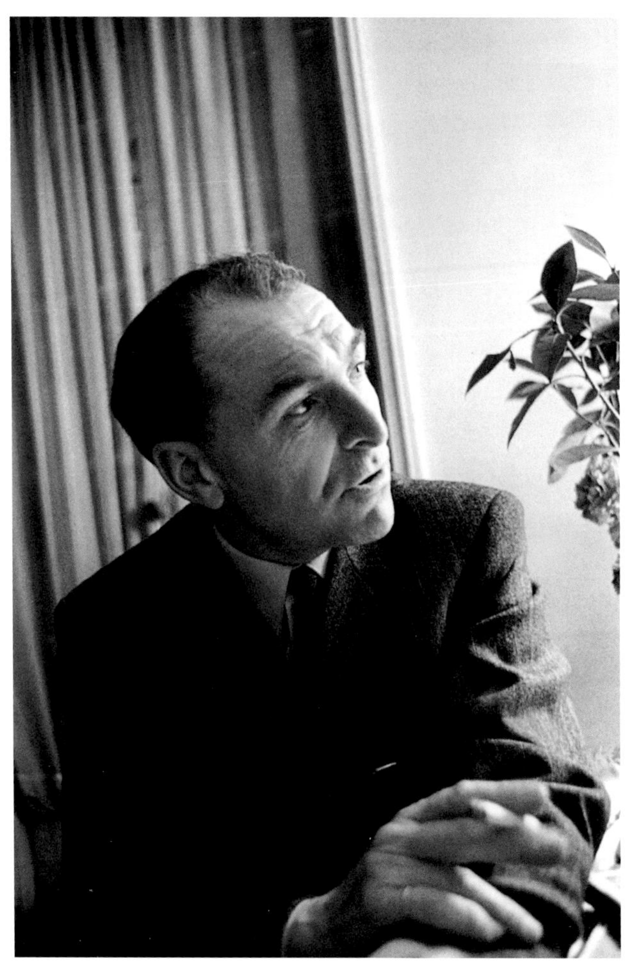

Robert Doisneau in New York, March 1966.

Introduction by JEAN-PAUL DUBOIS

PALM SPRINGS 1960 • Robert Doisneau

Flammarion

A remarkable man lived in Palm Springs ten years ago. A man of few words who liked to remain motionless for long periods of time so that he seemed sometimes to have been painted on canvas and stuck on the surface of the world. A man of old, retired from civil aviation, who landed here one day on the edge of a golf course and a desert, bought a modest home, and settled down with a large, lanky dog as yellow as it was blasé. In the middle of his living room this homeowner had built a large model in exact replica of his entire house. At the center of this small dollhouse was of course a living room with tiny sofas, a minuscule Labrador, a fake stone fireplace, in front of which stood a small painted plaster man who, within this shrunken world, seemed to contemplate a universe that intimidated him as much as it escaped him. And this is how, for years, this remarkable aviator lived out the rest of his life, jammed in a sunny corner like an old lizard looking fixedly at the frozen model of what must have been before, in this house, an old dream of sand and green grass.

As soon as I opened Robert Doisneau's album, as soon as I saw those buildings as artificial as the faces that lived in them, this grafted, gardened, decorated, sprinkled, and almost immediately evaporated world, I immediately thought that the fossilized man and his melamine dog would have had their place in this gallery of palm trees where, for lack of a shady eternity, each resident is still guaranteed 354 sunny days a year. And as I thought of this deceased aviator I slowly turned the album's pages until

I came across that captivating picture taken by Robert Doisneau in Palm Springs in November 1960, where we see a man in a white T-shirt taking pictures under a summer sky of a model of his house, the same house that can be seen, life-size, in the background (page 49). It looks like a delta wing. Or a half-finished gas station. Or a cable-car station. We know nothing about the busy, tanned man. Except that he furtively carries the calm features of a content homeowner, or the satisfied expression of a flattered architect. Confronted with this unsettling picture, I thought of course of the aviator and his yellowed dog. It seemed to me that the photos I was flicking through showed nothing more than the existence of men and women pinned to a giant model, a colored decor, like aging subjects wandering around a kind of American emirate within the folds of an age in the process of congealing before slowly disappearing, even as it was still busy rising from the ground.

Palm Springs first. What to say about this place except that from the beginning it carried the seeds of its own affliction. Even the native Cahuilla Indians of this valley found it difficult to bear the suffocating temperatures of the burning days piling up like bricks along the calendar. Everywhere and always the desert, with six pathetic inches of rain in good years at the very best. Yet America decided to settle in this cauldron, this oven of recooked sand. To spread, to entertain itself, to unfurl as it pleased. With, in the wake of its Eldorado Cadillacs and its Casino crooners, the dollar's chorale and its procession of green-grassed extravagances, architectural boastings, and expensive crazes. In 1960, Robert Doisneau confided in several letters his discomposure in discovering such a desert studded with nineteen golf courses drilled into the heart of this oven. What would he write today if he knew that this small town now counts one hundred and twenty-five? One hundred and twenty-five golf courses, 2,250 holes, or rather continually thirsty pits, which soak up 1.2 million gallons of water just to survive. And, as if all this were not enough, every deserving homeowner had to own a pool for each house. Sometimes even two. And when dinnertime came, while it was still over 95 degrees on the greens, the women dressed themselves in otter or mink furs, the better to bear the freezing blast from the air conditioners. Seeing this, knowing that, Doisneau could legitimately ask himself if he was on the other side of the world or at its end.

November 1960. Mercury brought out another model called the Comet. Charlton Heston received an Oscar for his role in *Ben Hur*. As for Eisenhower, he had not yet finished his term in office before he buried himself in the desert sands, of Palm Springs to be precise, among his friends, rich pensioners hooked on architecture as well as a few fortifying tonics and whom Frank Sinatra, Peter Lawford, and Ella Fitzgerald regularly came to entertain. The other Fitzgerald, Kennedy that is, was elected on the eighth of that month. Because it was him. And because on television Nixon, betrayed by his sweat glands, perspired far too much. Robert Doisneau arrived in New York with his cameras just a few days after this American electoral maelstrom. He was not there to photograph the new tenant of the White House but to fulfill a strange and particular mission. His old cellist friend Maurice Baquet, who accompanied him, noted that evening in his notebook: "Robert flew off to California somewhat displeased to learn that he first had to photograph the Palm Springs millionaires and Jerry Lewis in Hollywood."

What an odd idea! I am not talking about Lewis, but about Palm Springs. It was *Fortune*'s idea, the business magazine founded in 1930 by Henry Luce. Famous for its financial news, this newspaper was also acknowledged at the time for the quality of its pictures as much as for its excellent illustrators. Margaret Bourke-White, the famous war correspondent, and Walker Evans, the unflagging reporter of the Depression, collaborated, among others, on the elegant documenting of this scattered world. If Robert Doisneau's qualities and reputation amply justified the fact that he was employed in his turn, it is however the very nature of the subject he was entrusted with that is intriguing. To ask the most realist French photographer of his time—a suburbanite from the Montrouge suburb of Paris, brought up on silver salt and hyposulfite, a crusader of black and white—to carry out a color shoot of one of the most artificial towns in America, a chromium, golf-obsessed principality complete with colored lukewarm waters, banks, and arthritis is a surprising idea at the very least. In his memoirs Doisneau makes no mystery of his bewilderment in the face of the mission and the social world awaiting him: "Why have I been sent to Palm Springs, California? To take photos of golf. All I know is that you have to hit a small, white ball on green turf into a hole which is hardly big enough to receive it. . . . People come here from afar, even the palm trees come from Mexico, and the grass seeds, which tended to disperse with the wind at night, are now fixed to the ground by a rain of glue sprayed by helicopters." This is how his trip begins, with this distant, distrustful, unenthusiastic gaze for the scenery around him. It is also mocking: "I have been introduced to millionaire golf-players as 'Robert-from-Paris.'. . . I will have contacts in oil, cinema, and the automobile industry."

For the uninitiated, once he laid down his Rolleiflex camera, Robert Doisneau was someone who wrote wonderfully. In his letters to Maurice Baquet[1], in his memoirs and portraits[2], it takes only a few simple words for him to describe the world or a few lines to share his feelings during his American trip. It begins in the airplane: "Next to me sits a couple of good quality. The gentleman says to the lady 'I am rereading Pascal, one should always reread Pascal,' and so the lady replies, 'When I go to New York, I always break a finger nail.' I looked at the airplane's engines, but after four hours it gets tedious." Sitting in a restaurant on the way back from the golf course a few days later, things are no better: "At the end of the evening it is as if I have blurred vision, and this morning my tongue is white, feeling melancholy with their confiture they put on steak, it upsets the digestion." This can of course be read as the caricatured complaints of a Frenchman obliged for far too long to forego his braised steak, but this would considerably reduce its author's focus, as he also knew how to read American semantics perfectly and to dissect its intimate sociology. Still in Palm Springs. One evening on the way back from work, confronted with the beauty of the fading light that always enthralled him without ever blinding him:

> On the land bordering the greens, houses resembling Swiss chalets or Chinese pagodas had been built, like so many fantasies and memories of traveling. Inside, old, very rich couples slowly bored themselves. On the terraces, flags floated on masts bearing the emblem of a cup or a glass; a pleasant way of inviting those suffering from loneliness in the neighborhood for whiskey or coffee. Pools everywhere of course. Pools without dives or splashes. I remember a despondent seventy-year-old who had achieved his life's dream: having worked with four telephones in his office, he now owned not one but two pools separated by a mirror. One for the summer and one for the winter, the latter went into the living room. His rheumatism began the day he entered the water. Sitting in his armchair in front of the azure blue mirror, he pushed rubber ducks around with a long bamboo cane.

And there we are. You have hardly opened this book and you already know its contents. A few hastily written notes in the photographer's notebook are enough to outline all the pictures that follow, to situate them, to give them life and volume. A Robert Doisneau photograph of America is never a simple illustration, but rather the superposition of an infinite number of details, notes, feelings, thoughts, and observations that are often invisible separately to the naked eye but that merge, overlap, and always end by giving an aesthetic but also hypercritical and pertinent view of this small world of palm trees and glued greens.

Throughout this California trip we feel that Robert Doisneau was embarrassed by the very essence of this continent, by these men and women who in some ways resembled him and yet in whom he could never recognize himself. Despite a few flashes of sympathy, he seems ill at ease, and all his notes from that period confirm his critical distance and confused feelings:

> Dimension must not be confused with harmony, the Americans have not understood this, I mean in general. . . . I feel as if I belong to another age, like a Louis XV armchair in an airfield or a cello in front of the Life building. . . . I felt like the specimen of a population living west of the old Europe, speaking a dying idiom, in whom a few ethnologists recognize however a small talent for making pictures full of an old-fashioned charm but who finds it difficult to adapt to the big Hollywood

machine. This is what those who made me cross the Atlantic to share their games must have thought.

The editors of *Fortune* in the 1960s probably did not have the same artistic ambitions as their predecessors. The commission was motivated by other more pragmatic concerns: the celebration of Palm Springs and publicity for it as "the World Capital of Winter Golf." By hiring Robert Doisneau to achieve their ends, the New York editors thought they were simply employing the talents of a remarkable casual illustrator. Little did they know that they had just enlisted a subtle and conscientious testifier who was to draw up, day after day, roll after roll, an inventory of the ostentatious and extravagant American way of life. With skillful commercial rhetoric *Fortune* therefore published an article entitled "Grass and Pleasure Grow in the Desert." Composed of a selection of twenty-three relatively banal photographs where fashionable cocktail shots mix with golfing compositions, their work was far from doing justice to the clinical and joyful perspicacity with which the French photographer carried out his contract. This *Palm Springs 1960* brings together all the other pictures that the magazine disregarded. Some are real masterpieces—in particular those on pages 88 and 89—which seem to come straight from the studio of a melancholic Hopper or a meticulous Peellaert as he added the final touches to his Las Vegas–themed

The Big Room. A harsh light seems to fall from the sky, and the ravaged faces seem to rise up from hell. It is a little like showing the other side of the picture, the end of the game, the last of the eighteenth hole and a taste of the nineteenth. Palm Springs in 1960? A twilight time, a strange feeling like the gift of a new world dedicated to the whims of old demanding rich people.

This book by Robert Doisneau, the travel book of a colorized epic, also asks a question of a different kind. At what point does an era cease to exist? How can the first signs of decline be recognized? Perhaps when we no longer recognize the make of the automobiles in the photos. Or when a bunch of guys dressed in pale jersey pose in front of tiled pools with big cigars in their mouths. Or again, when we gaze this way and that but all we see is a totally, radically, scrupulously white America. Not one person of color, not one Latino, not one Asian in Palm Springs. Only Caucasians. Another kind of Indian reservation. A tribe without a superego. Which waters sand, lives in refrigerators, builds big houses to hold smaller ones, and digs pools with celluloid swans floating on the surface.

So in this desert, confronted with this strange and fascinating shower of pictures from our parents' or grandparents' time, it is right to ask sometimes if this town, this racial fantasy, this ethnic and clinical composition ever really existed? Did Doisneau photograph a mirage? This world with its unique "59" Holiday Inn, its famous Riviera Hotel, its eccentric villas, which housed Sinatra, Bob Hope, Gene

Autry, and Dinah Shore when they were not at the Chi Chi Club drinking multicolored cocktails, the world we catch a glimpse of here, that we almost touch with memories we never had, has disappeared for ever. Swallowed up by sprinkled waters. Evaporated into the desert air. But another just as voracious and radical world has taken its place, still and forever sucking up the aquifers, turfing over hells, filling up liners and probably—as of old—still hating splashes just as much.

Now it is enough to turn the pages and allow for the pictures to tell their detailed story of that Californian Fall in 1960, while these people, pars, irons, and frames mix in latitude 33°49′26″ north and longitude 116°31′49″ west, at exactly 479 feet above sea level.

Automobiles of course, parking lots obviously, women in shorts, men in carts, extravagant stone railings, and everywhere lawns, palm trees, growing or full-grown, sprouting insolent and shaggy like hair implants. And then imperceptibly, the objective leaves the gardens and closes in on the hive, into the honey of the homes, revealing the intimacy of these trophy-houses, never foraging but simply giving and describing each thing's place, for we quickly understand that here each thing must remain in its place. Once finished with his inventory of interior decoration, Doisneau turns his camera on his hosts. And often his meticulous, attentive, faithful work resembles the precious paintings of old. Somber canvases with floating faces taken during parties at the heart of this fresh aristocracy of dollars, where evening furs rub shoulders with old marquis, the smell of fresh cigars, Rubinstein perfume, and the clinking of bourbon in crystal bowls. The best of the business world is presented to the camera. The president of the Superior Oil Company William Keck Jr.'s scowling face. The ex-boss of National Distillers Eric Stainton's informal cashmere jersey. Lew Parrish, in charge of the truck drivers' trade union and his strong whiskey. And Mrs. Henry Dodge's bathing suit (page 60). The blue corrugated "one-piece" bathing suit in which she poses, telephone in hand, in front of the counter of the Bruno tennis store. In front of Mrs. Dodge is a huge table of hors d'oeuvres of the "all you can eat" variety. She ignores the food and shelters from the neon lights under a hat wrapped with a creamy scarf. She embodies something of her era, a social status, a style, a body, an elegantly vulgar, sexy charm. She is visibly posing. She is there. She remains there. She looks at the photographer. She seems to see only him.

Finally, the swimming pools. There are just enough pools for us to understand the decorative role they hold in this designed city. Yet where it could be thought they would bring a refreshing air to things, these waterholes empty of any swimmers and thereby empty of reason, with their surfaces smoothed over by absence and boredom, resound like a depressing mantra reminding us of Robert Doisneau's words: "Pools without dives or splashes. . . . His rheumatism began the day he entered the water."

Fortunately there is all the rest of it, the hugeness of American nature, the texture of the sand, the nuanced skies, the excessive angles, each picture's immensity seeming to offer impossible views. When the sun's rays weakened and the shadows stretched at the end of the day, Doisneau, the absorber of light, did not deny himself some pleasure: "I am beginning to understand what soft colors are. . . . Since my arrival in Palm Springs it is delightful, especially in the evening—verdigris façades, orange-colored rooftops, and lilac-colored palm trees, there are other combinations of course, but they are all entrancing." And this is how the album ends, peacefully on two fading days, two golden twilights that leave the city as it is, golf courses and men tucked away until tomorrow, all seen from above, probably from the top of an Indian mountain, streets and houses lit by watts, glowing all over the hollowed valley, sinking softly into the darkness that precedes the night.

Jean-Paul Dubois, December 2009

Journalist, Jean-Paul Dubois became a reporter for *Le Nouvel Observateur* in 1984. His travel writing on the United States was published in two volumes: *L'Amérique m'inquiète* (1996) and *Jusque-là tout allait bien en Amérique* (2002). He has also written several novels including *Une vie française* (2004), published in English by Vintage.

[1] *J'attends toujours le printemps,* Actes Sud, 1996.
[2] *À l'imparfait de l'objectif,* Actes Sud, 2001.

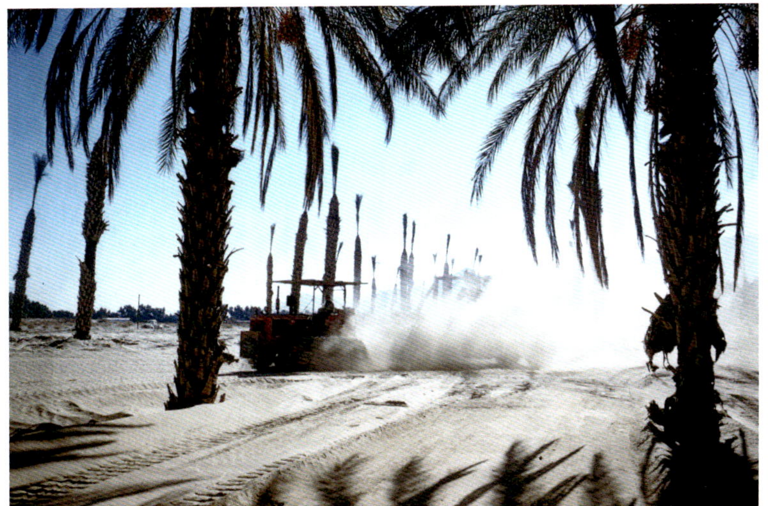

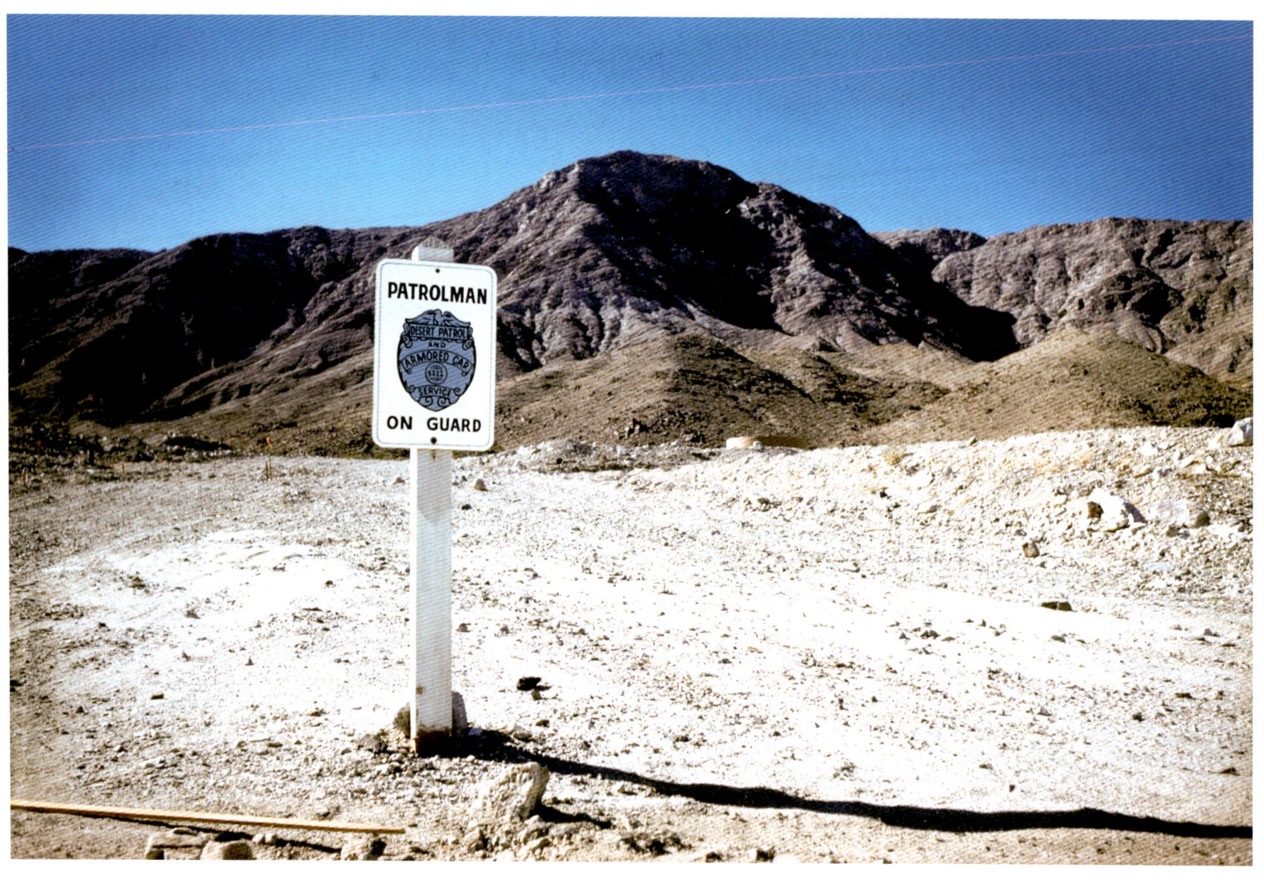
PATROLMAN
DESERT PATROL
AND
ARMORED CAR
SERVICE
ON GUARD

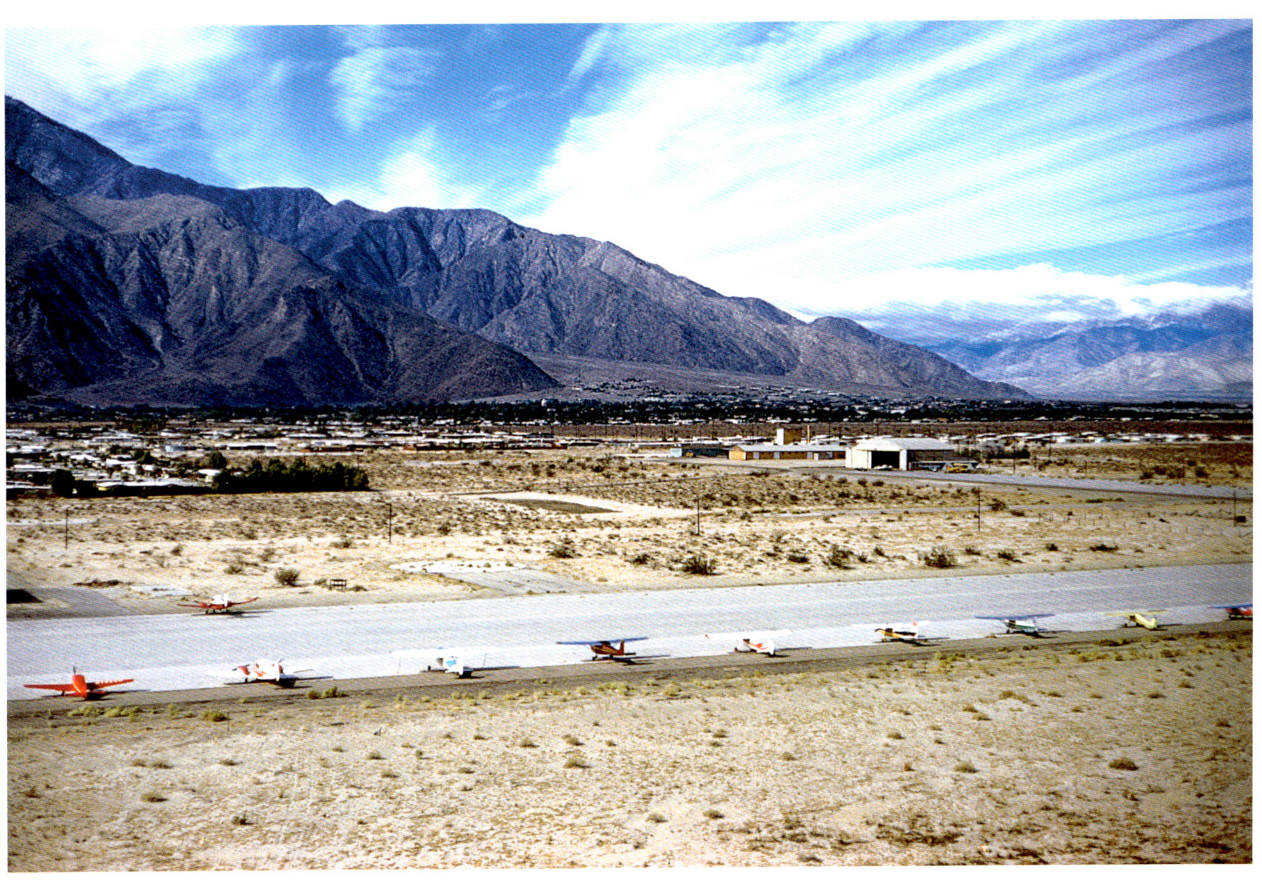

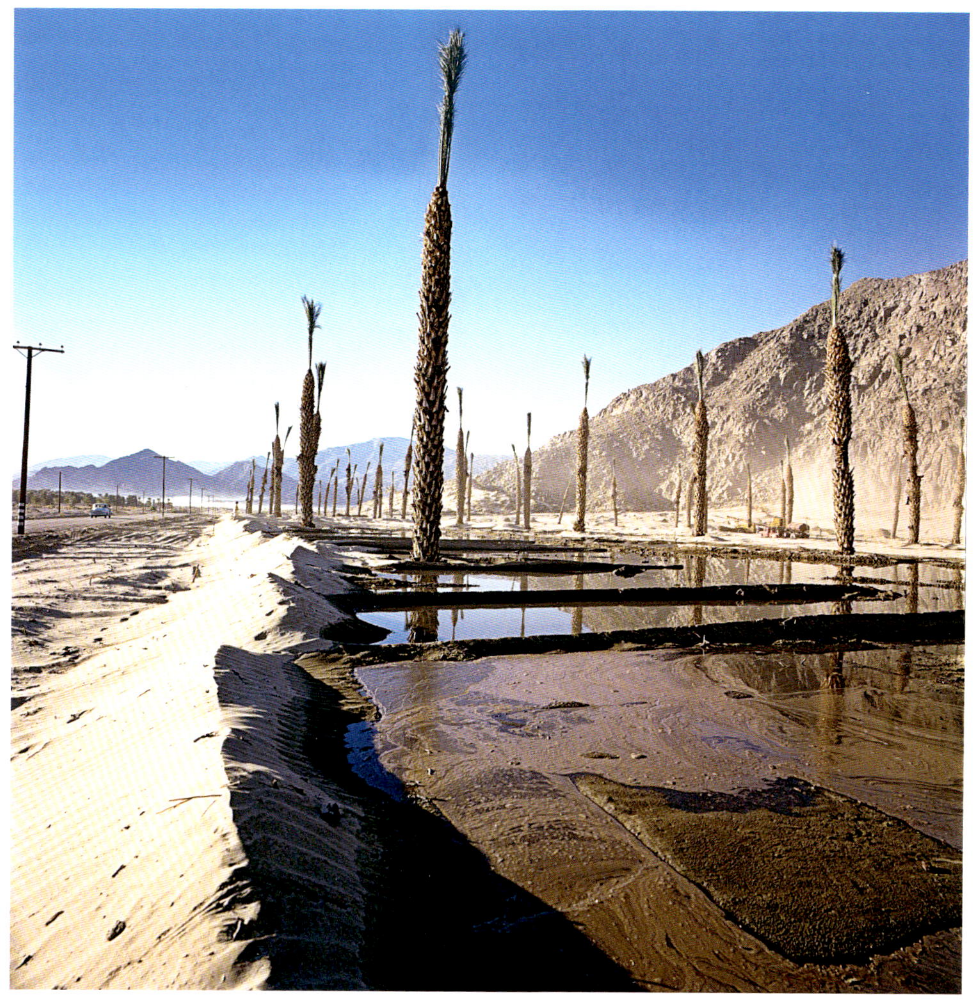

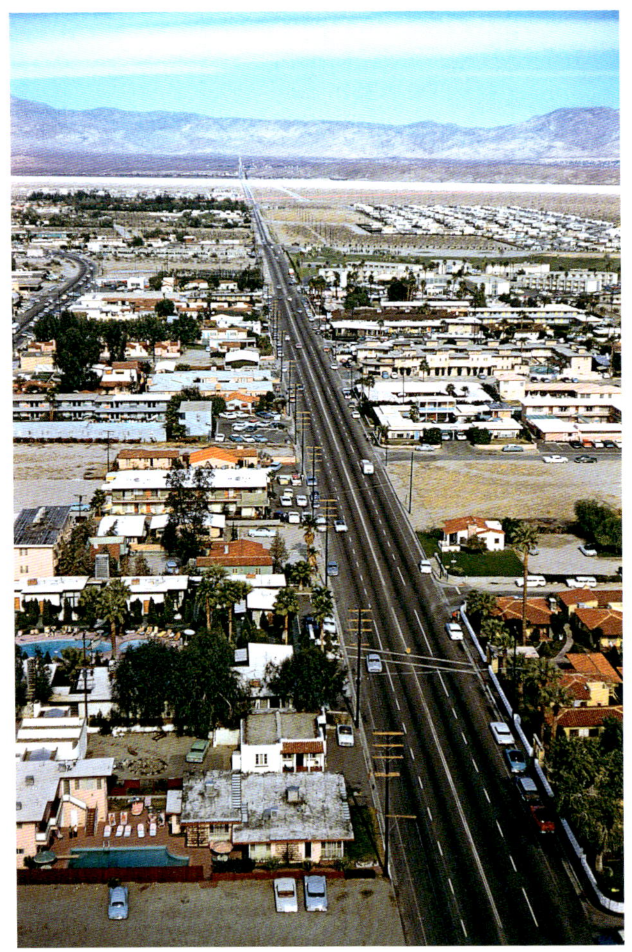

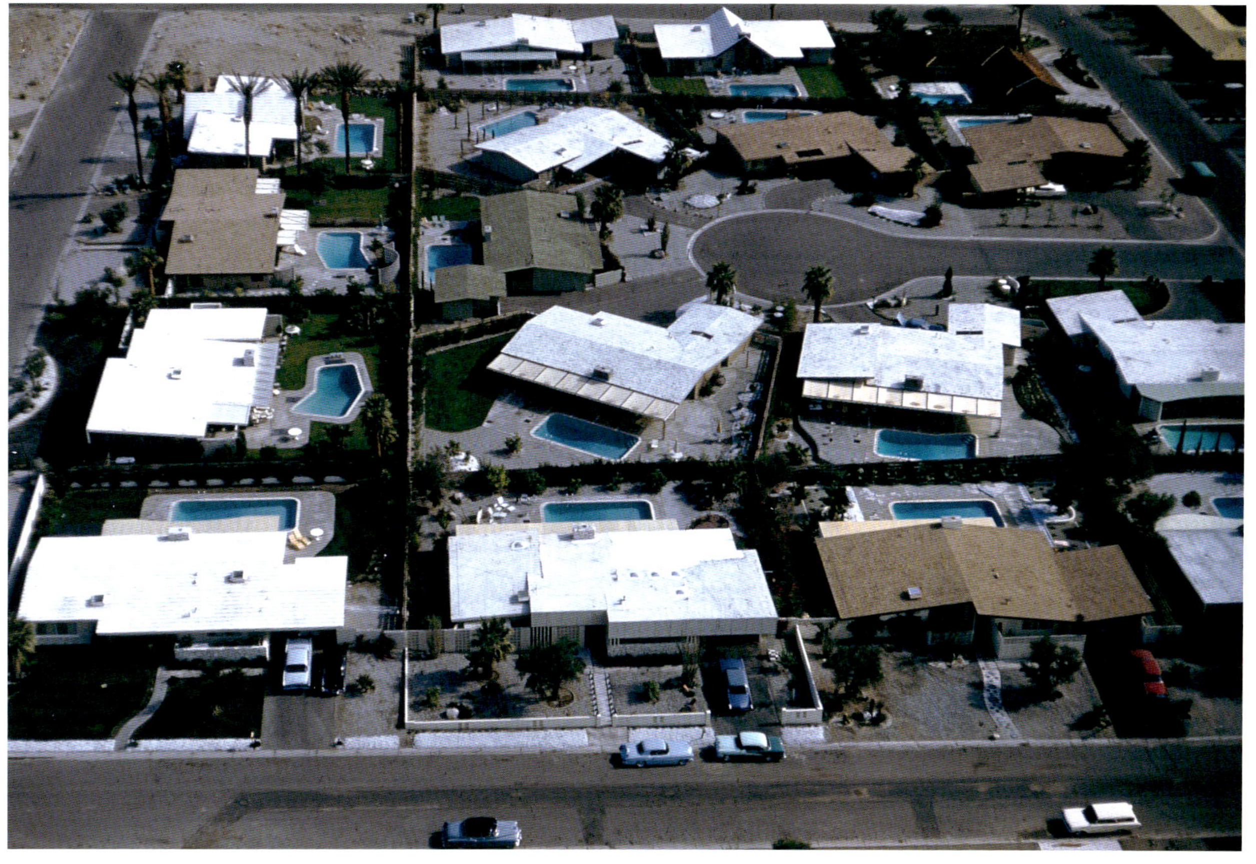

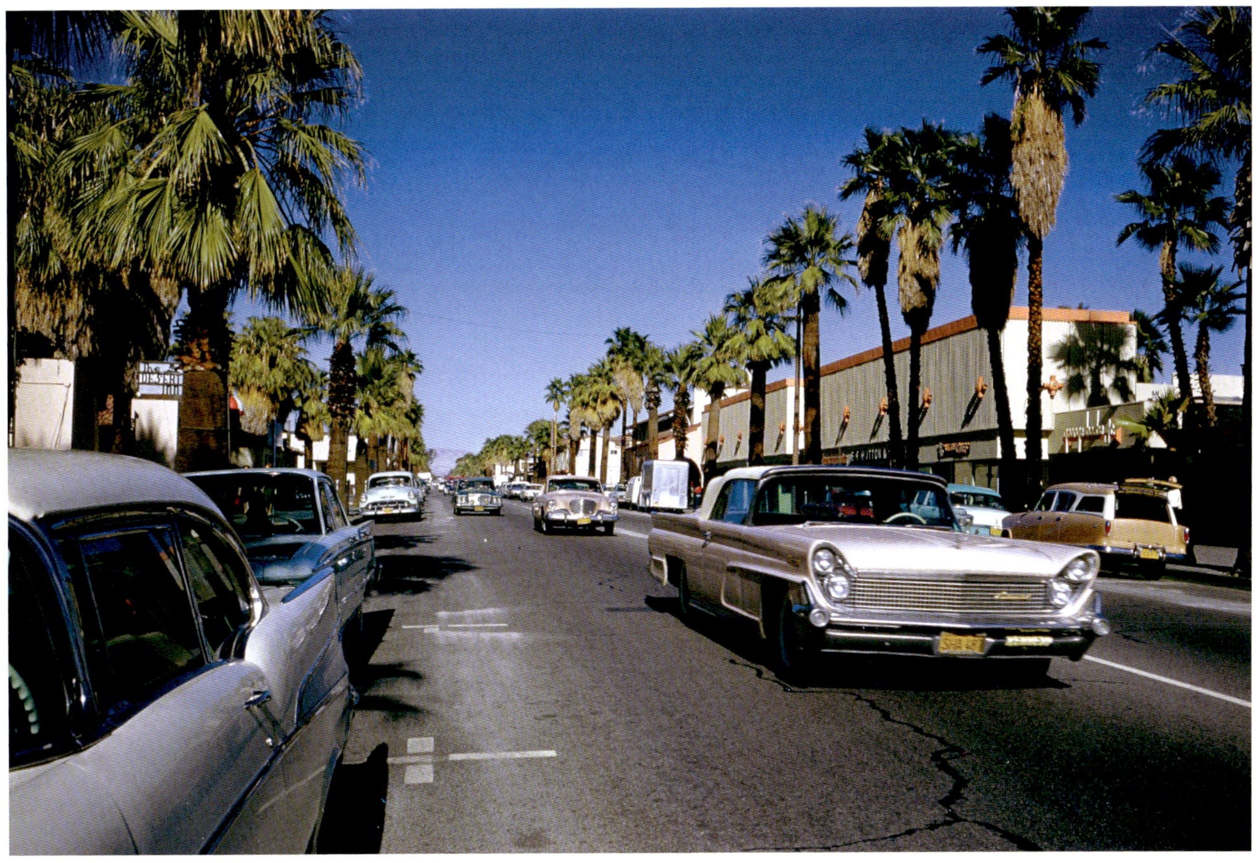

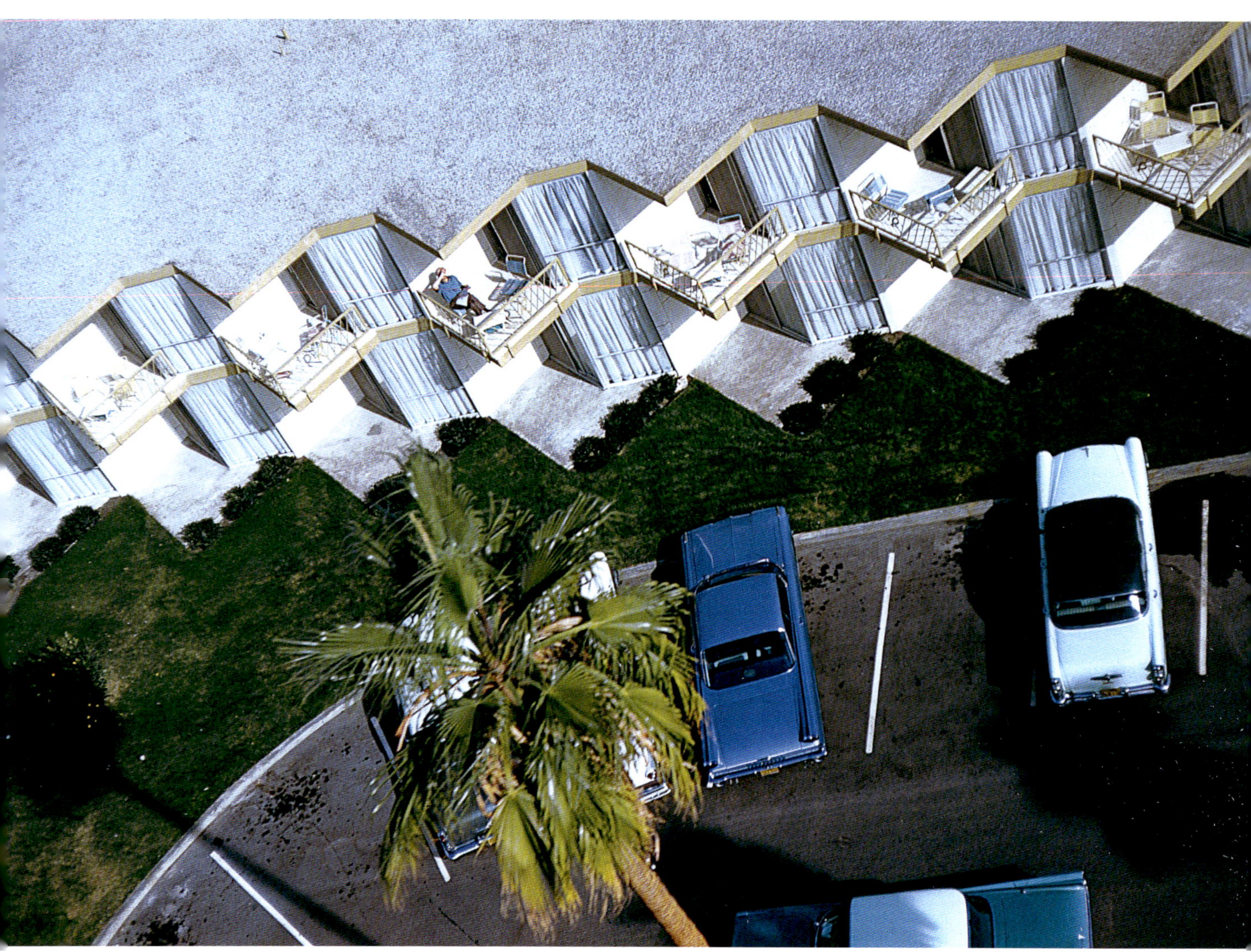

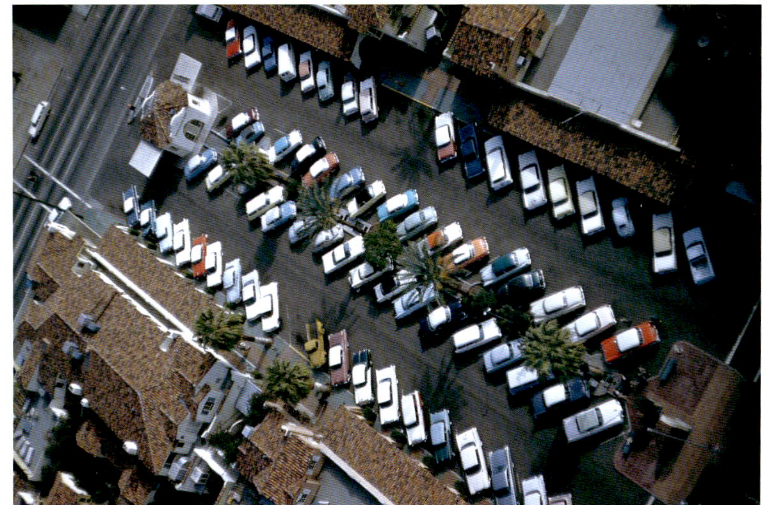

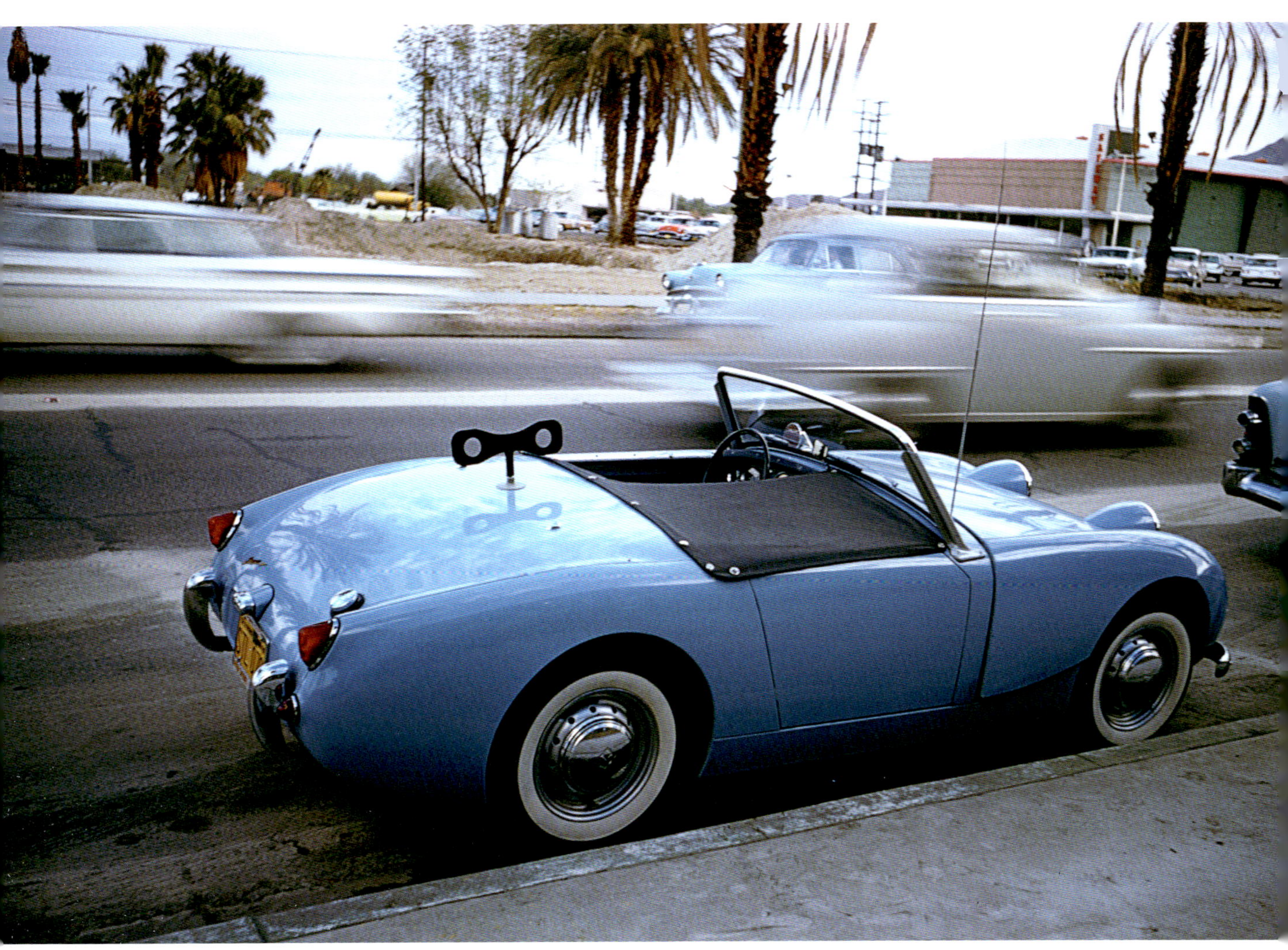

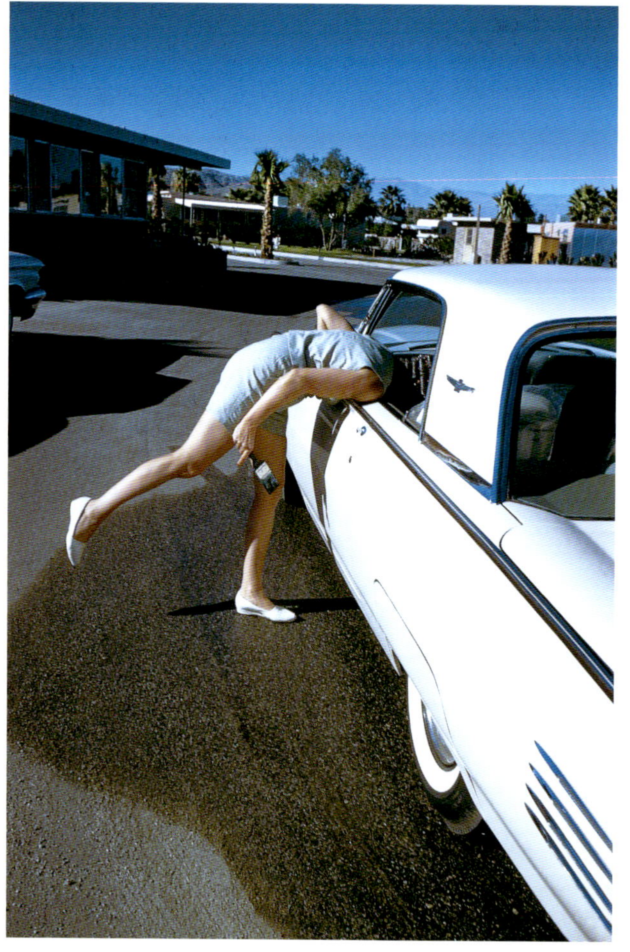

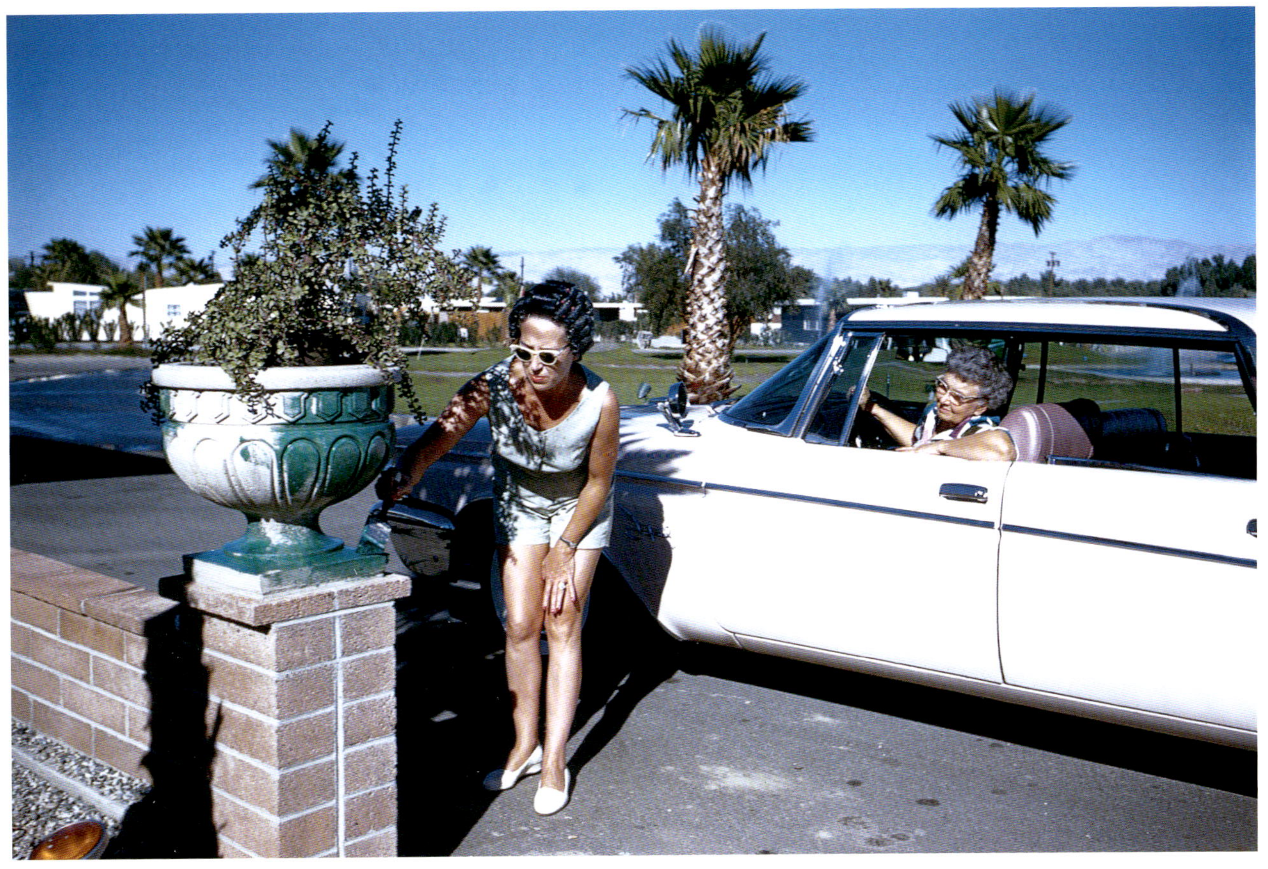

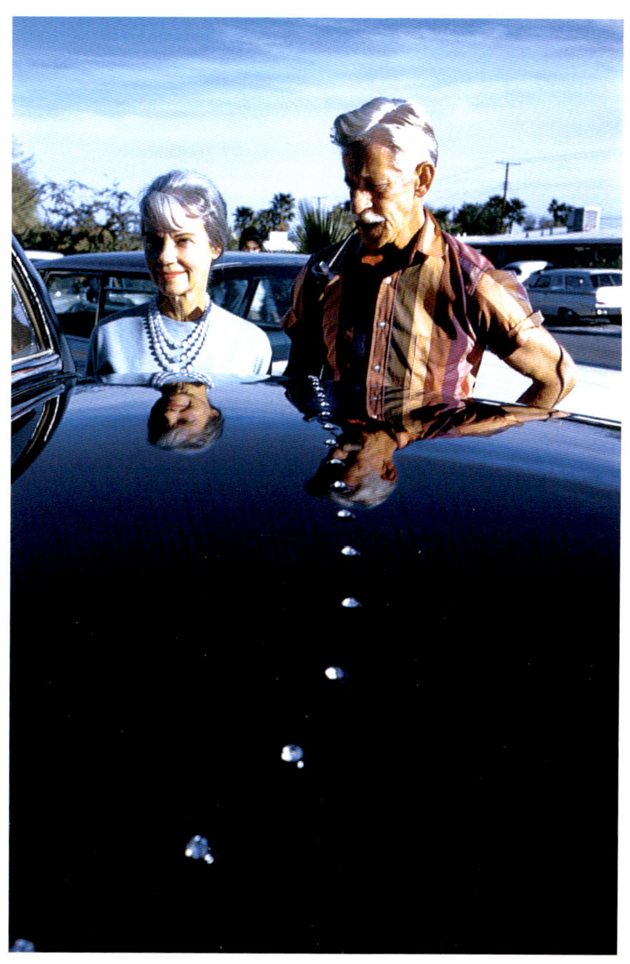

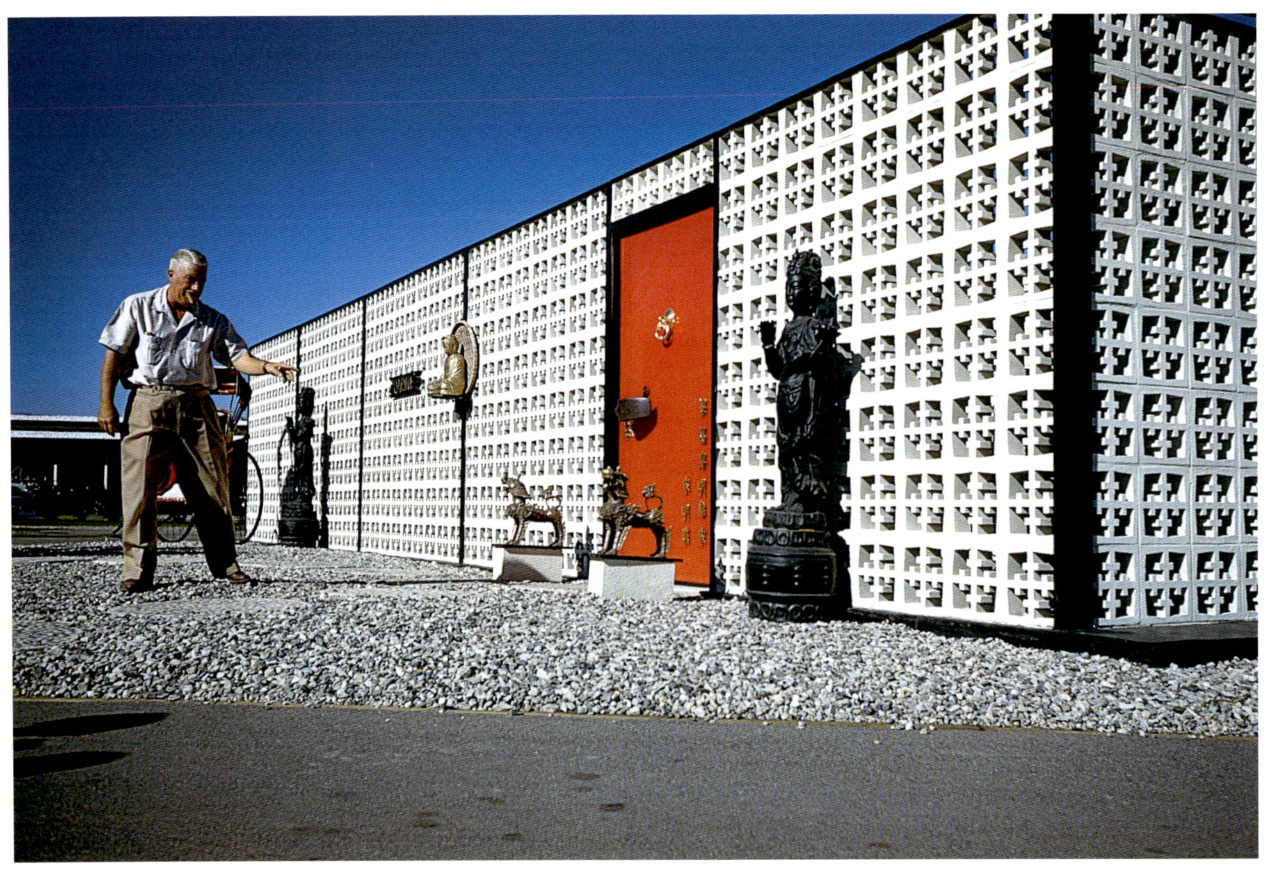

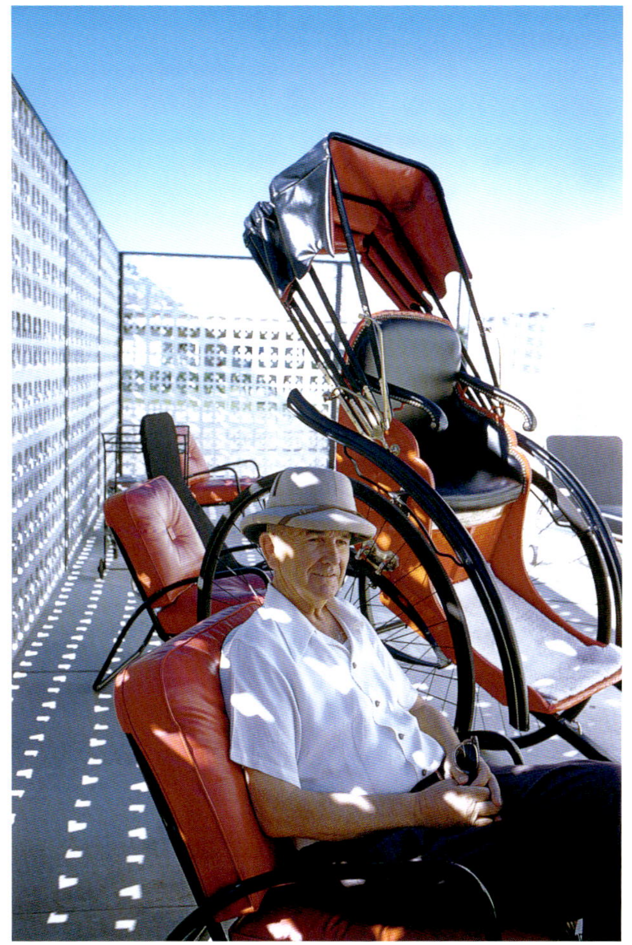

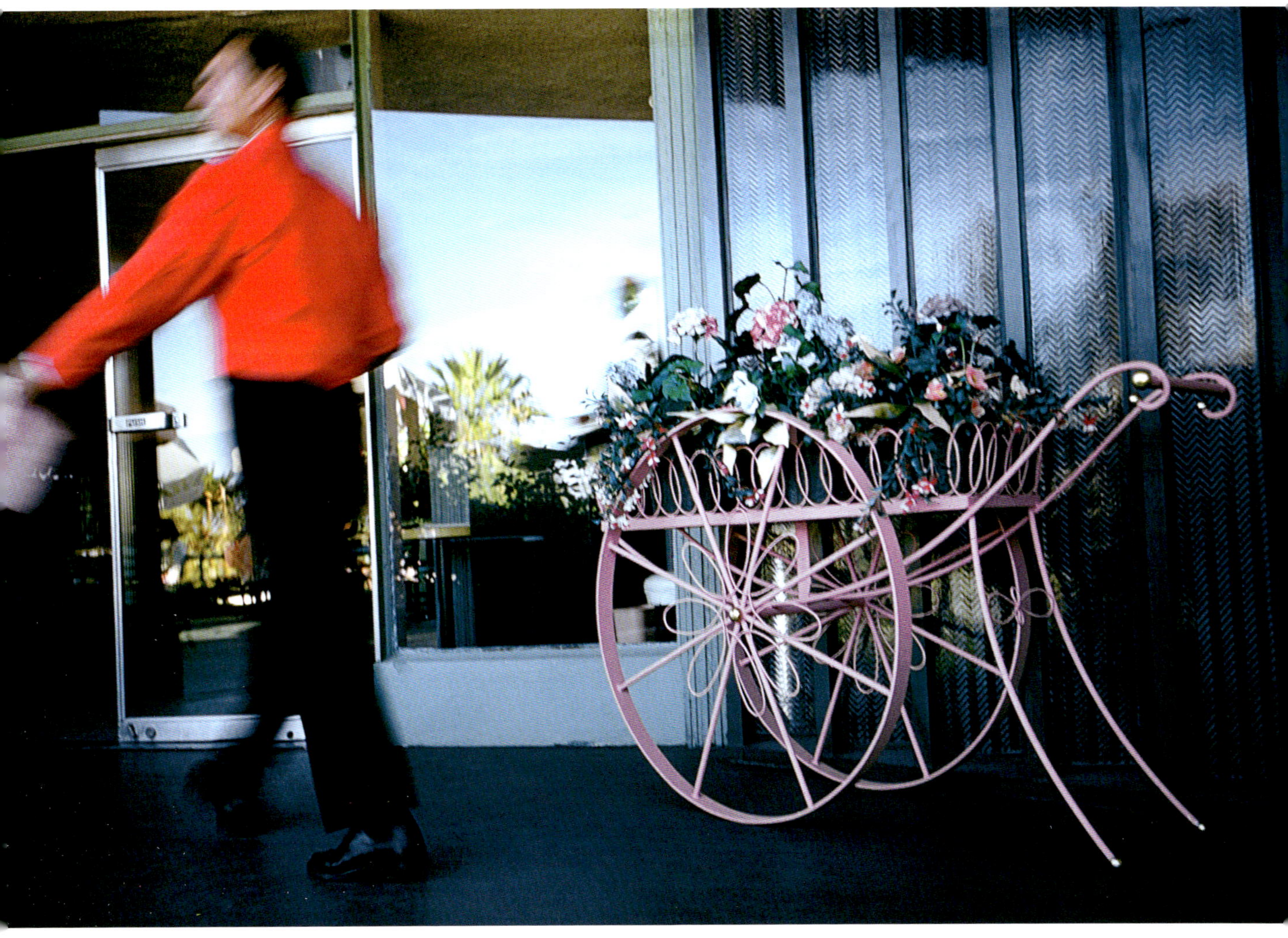

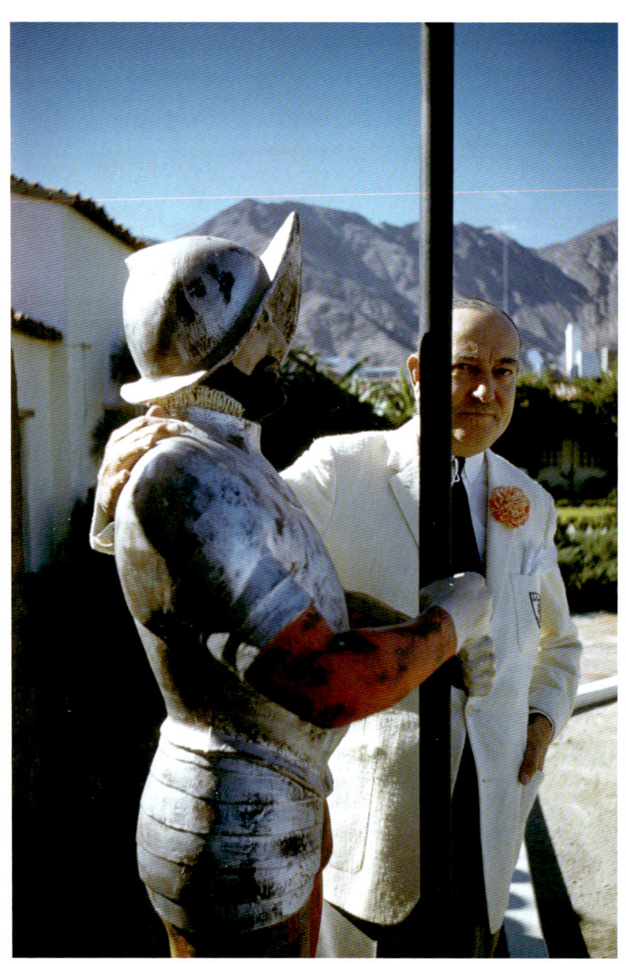

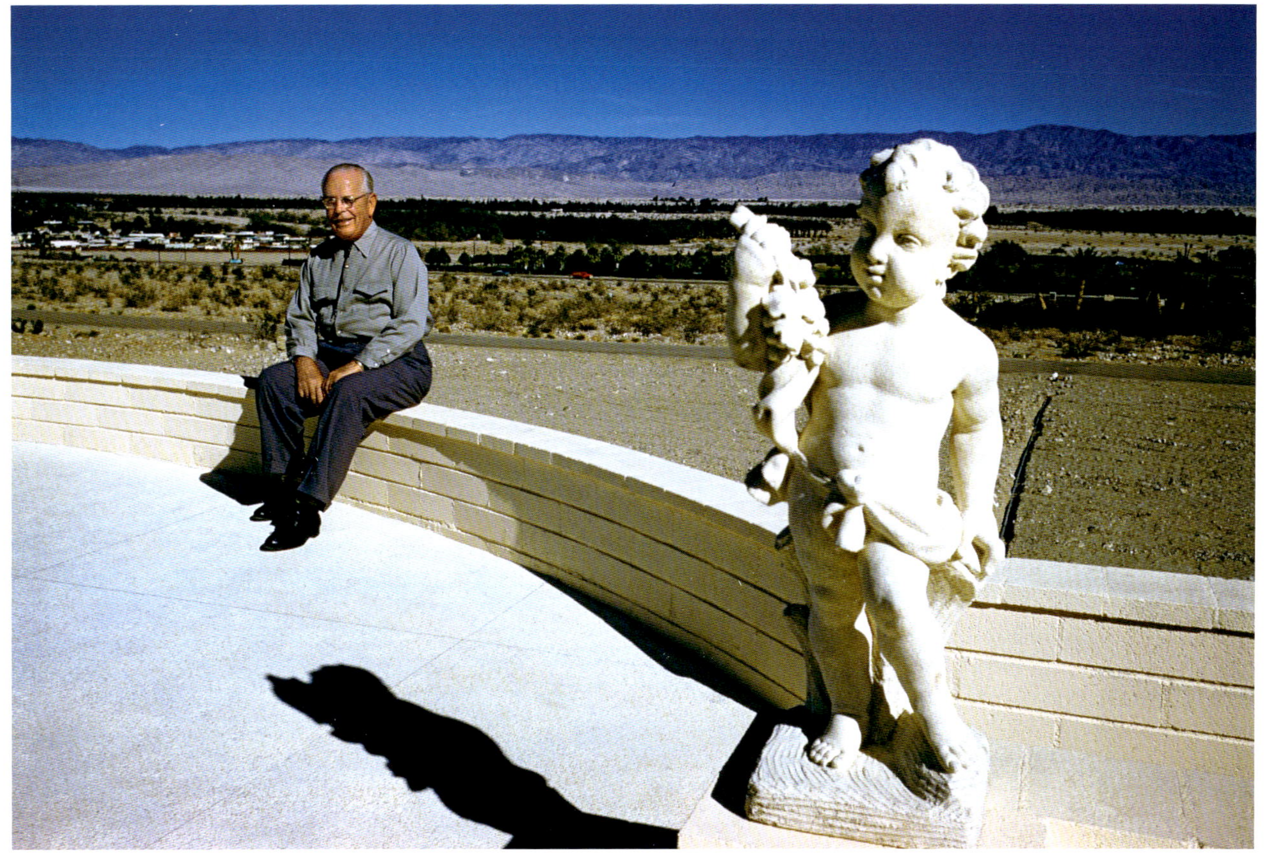

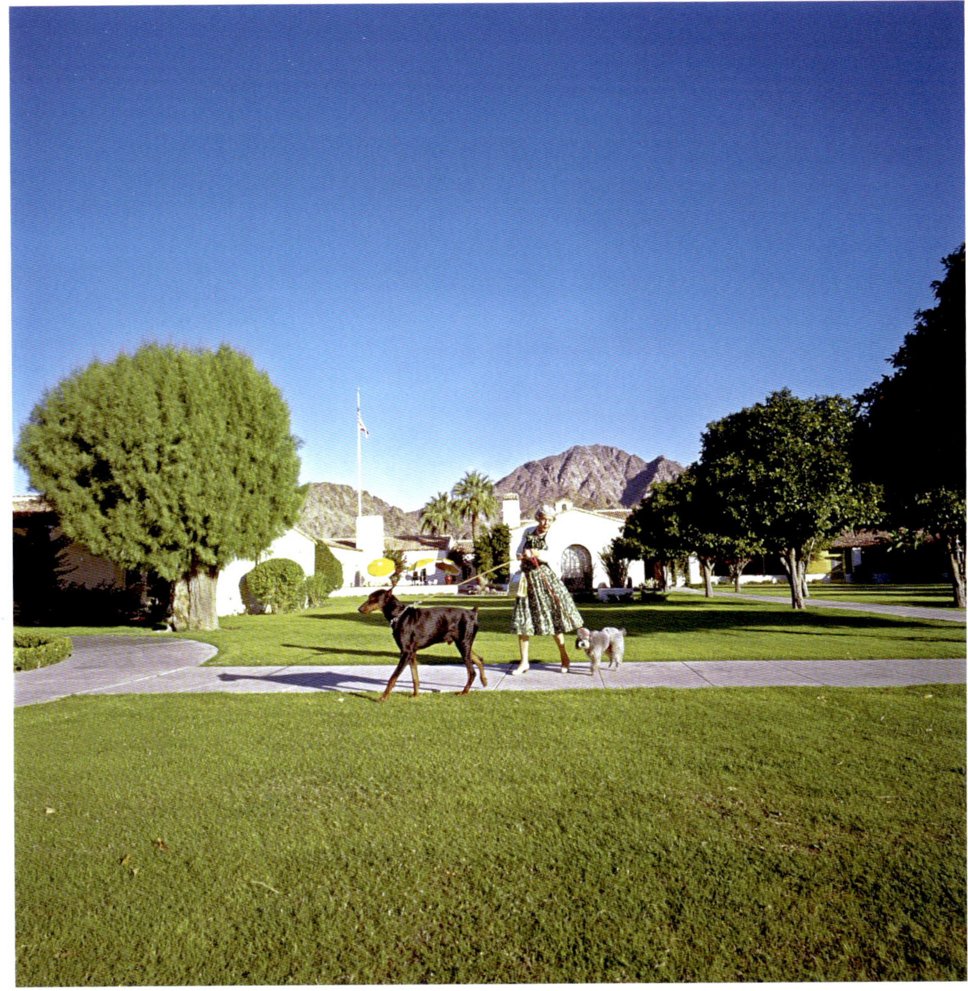

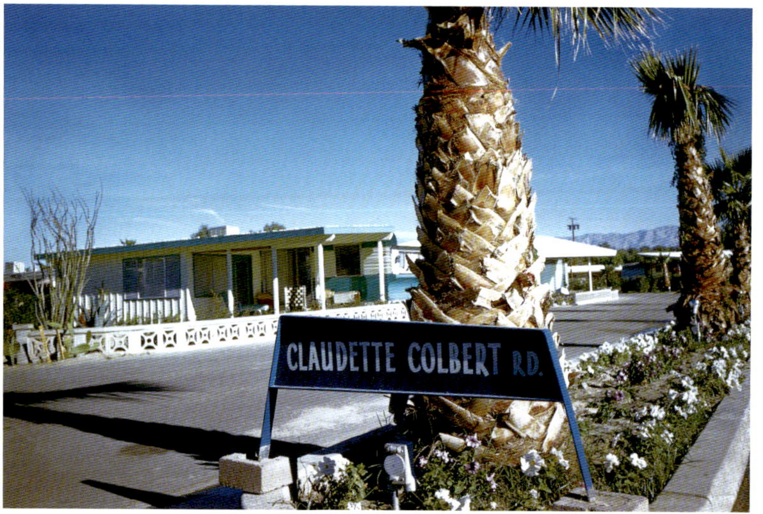
CLAUDETTE COLBERT RD.

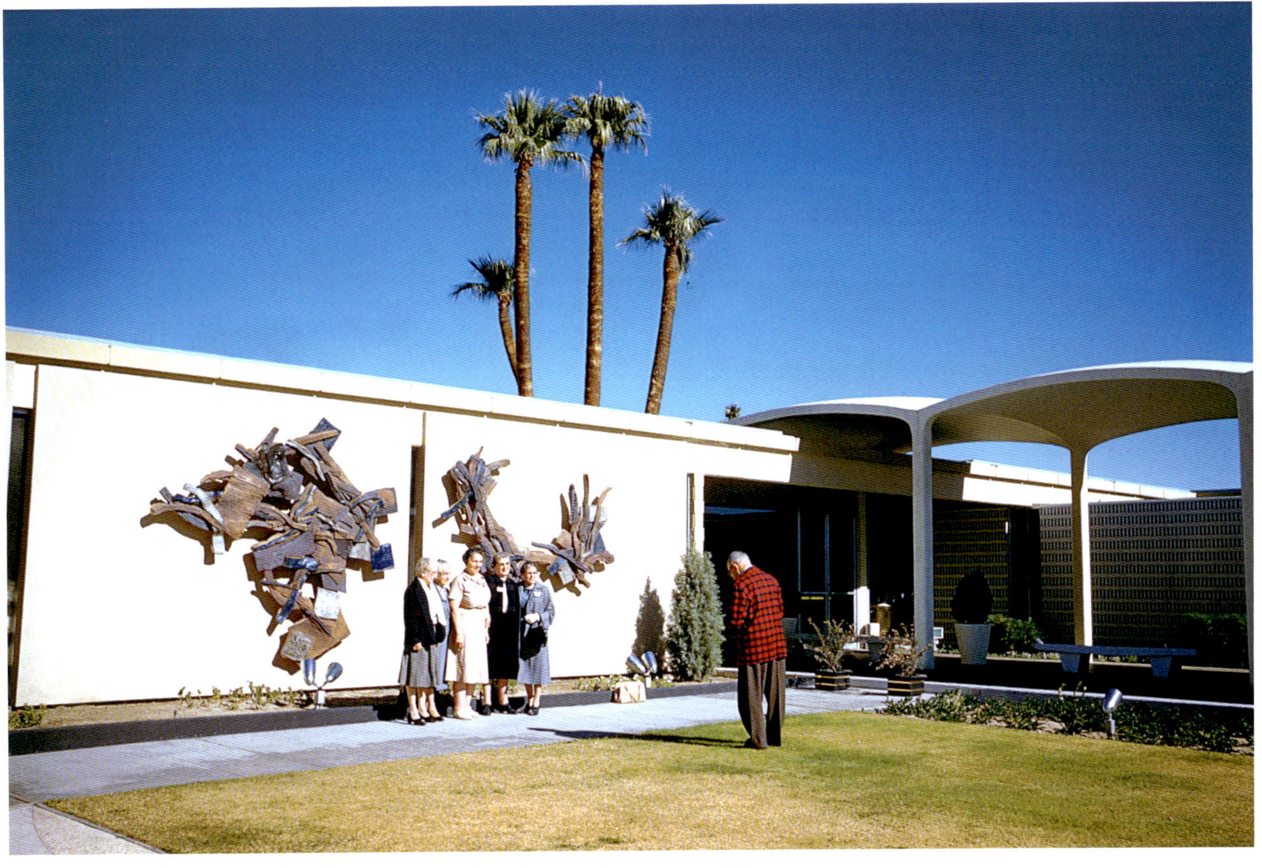

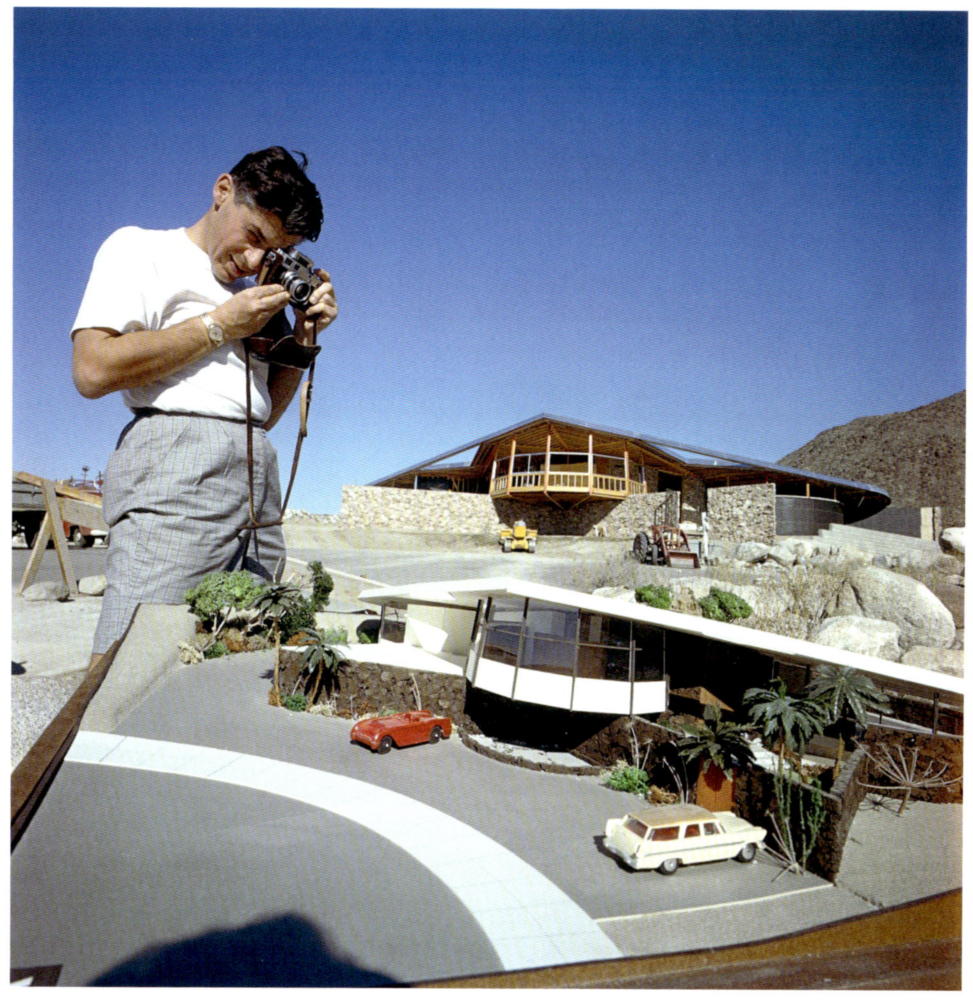

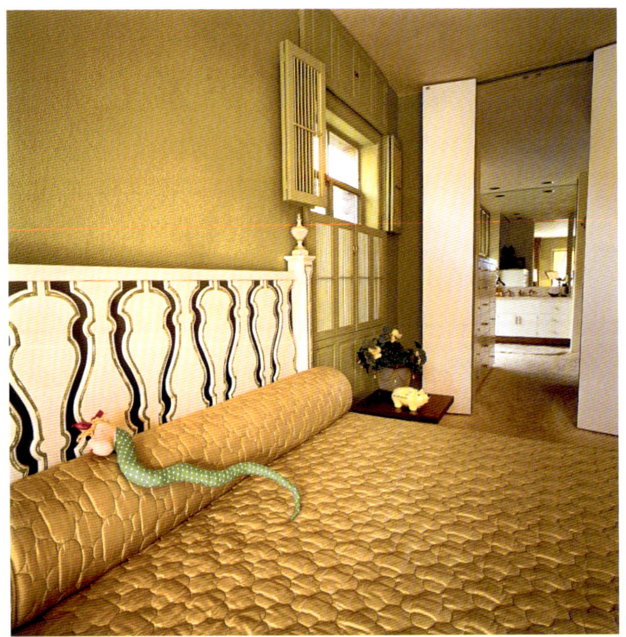

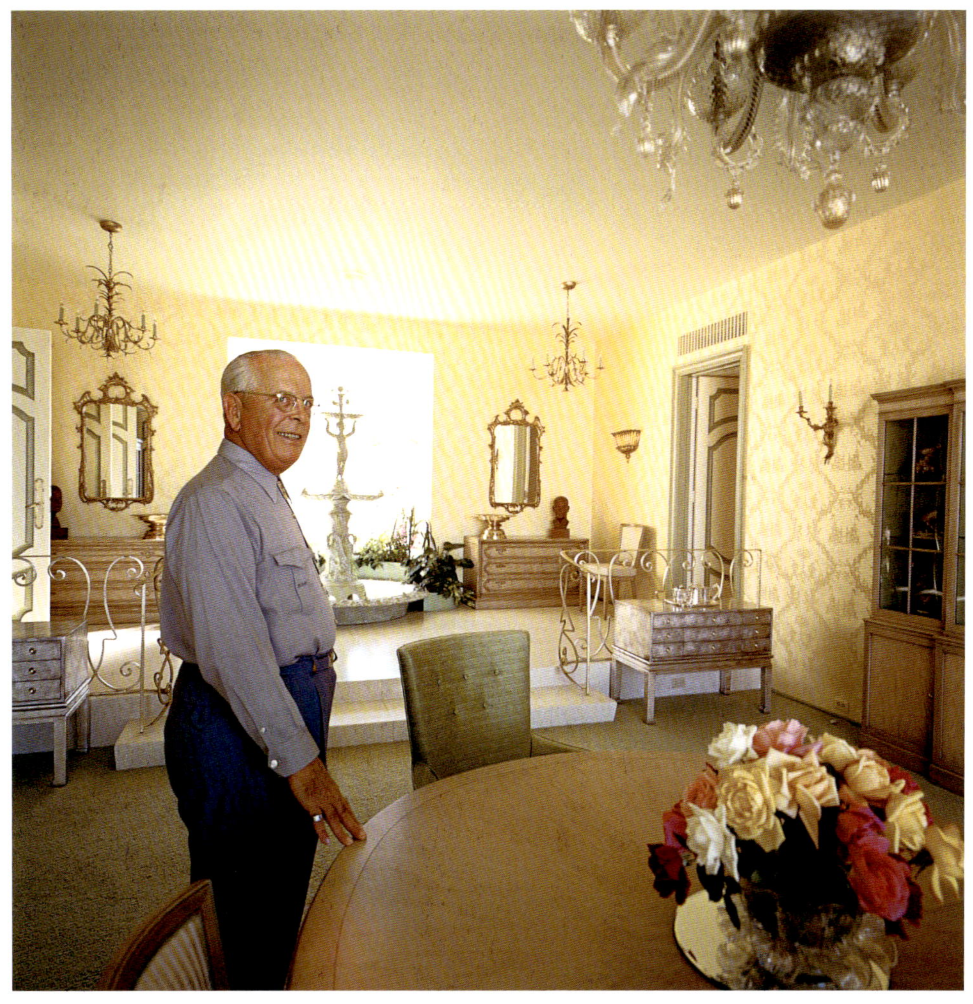

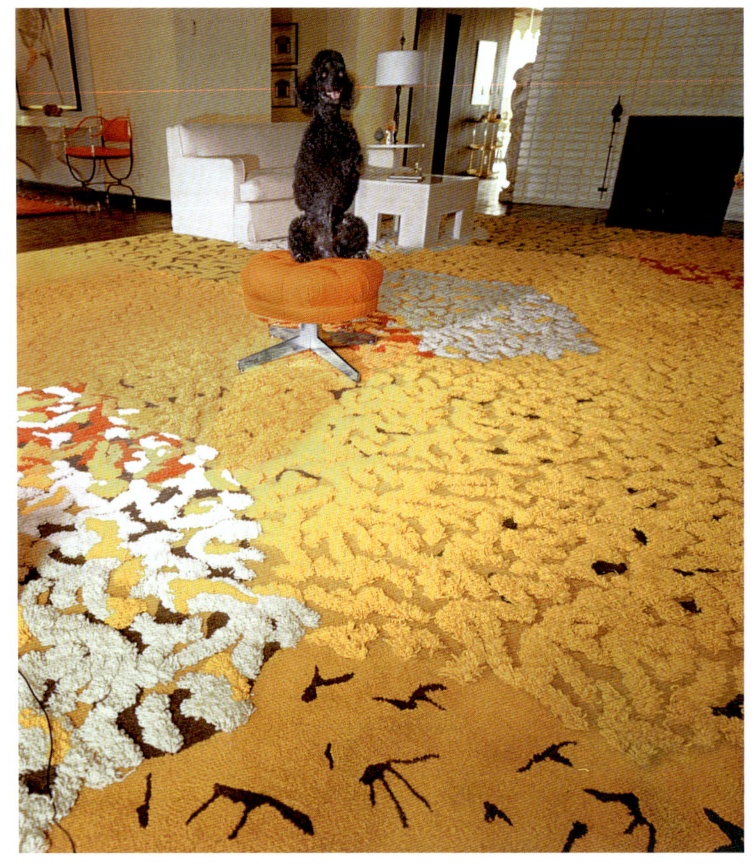

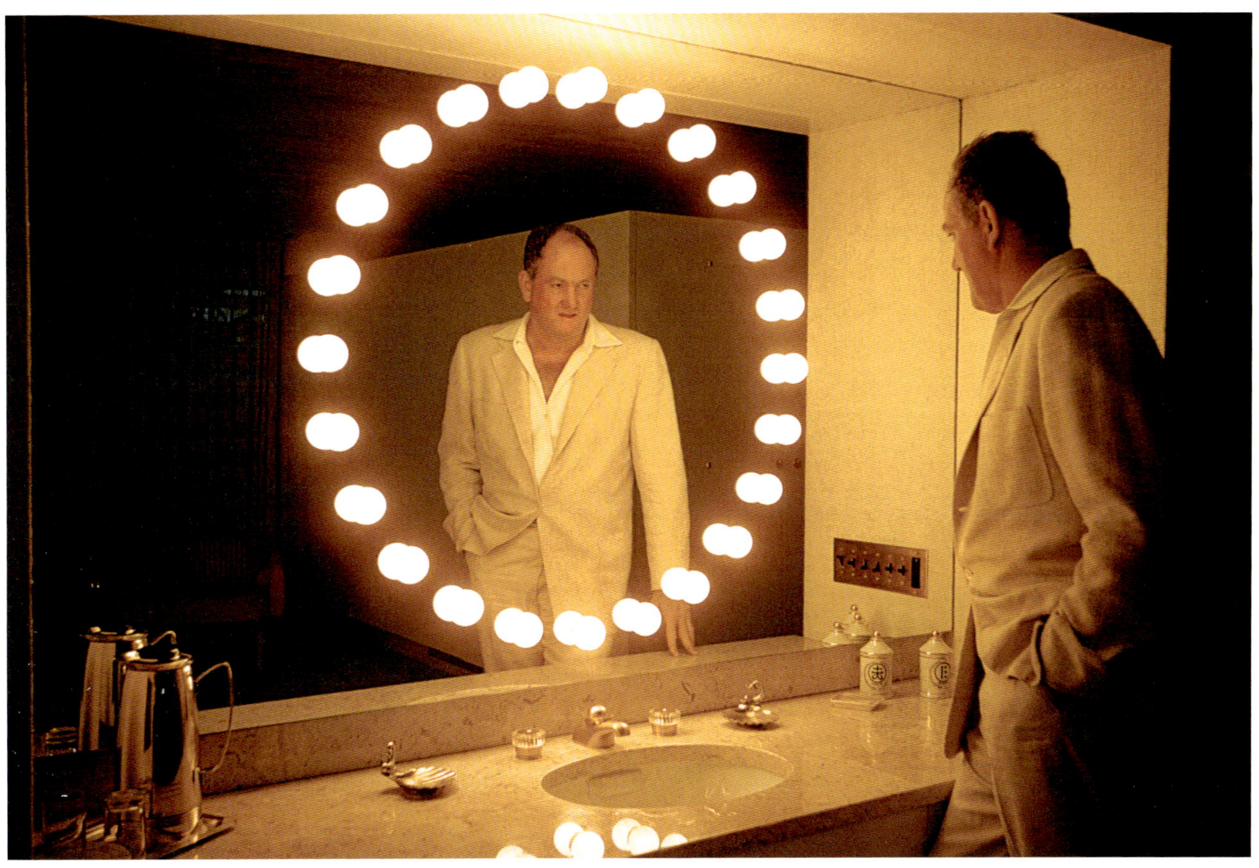

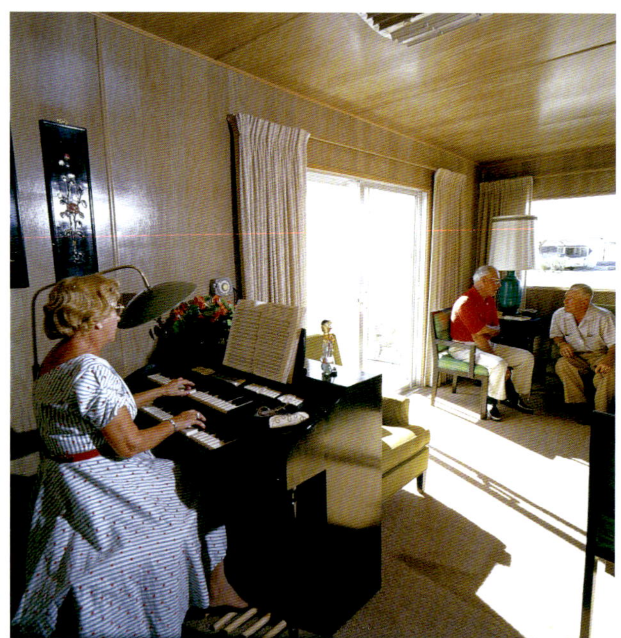

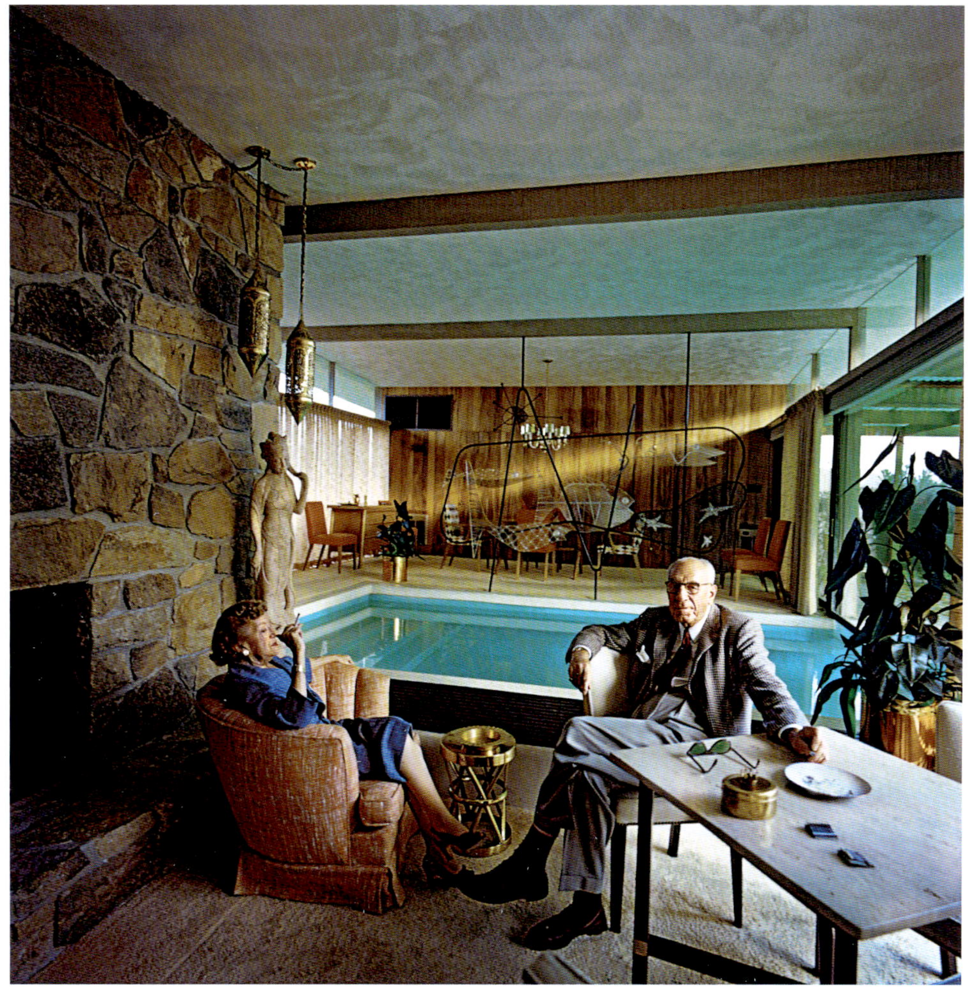

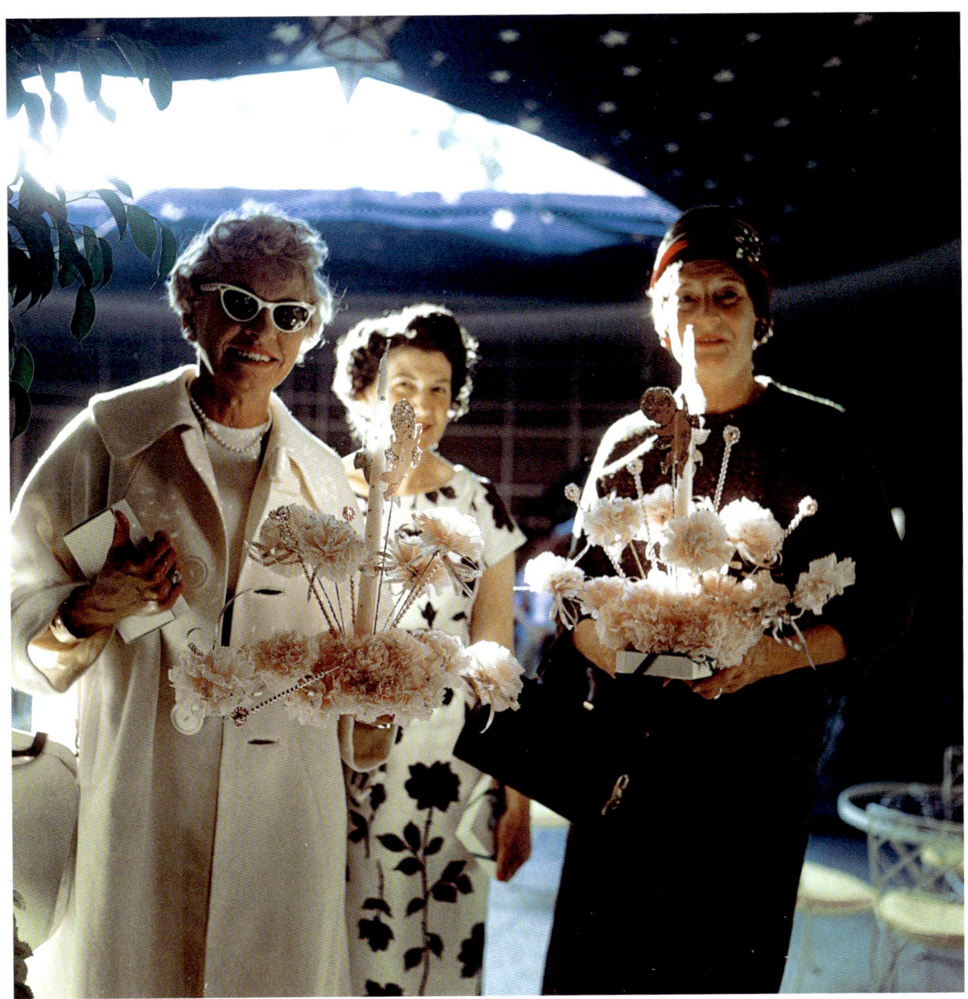

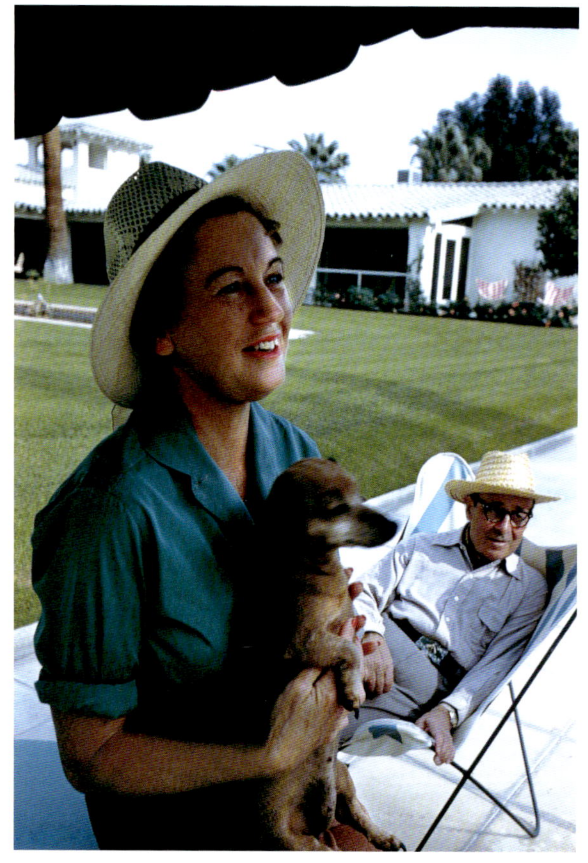

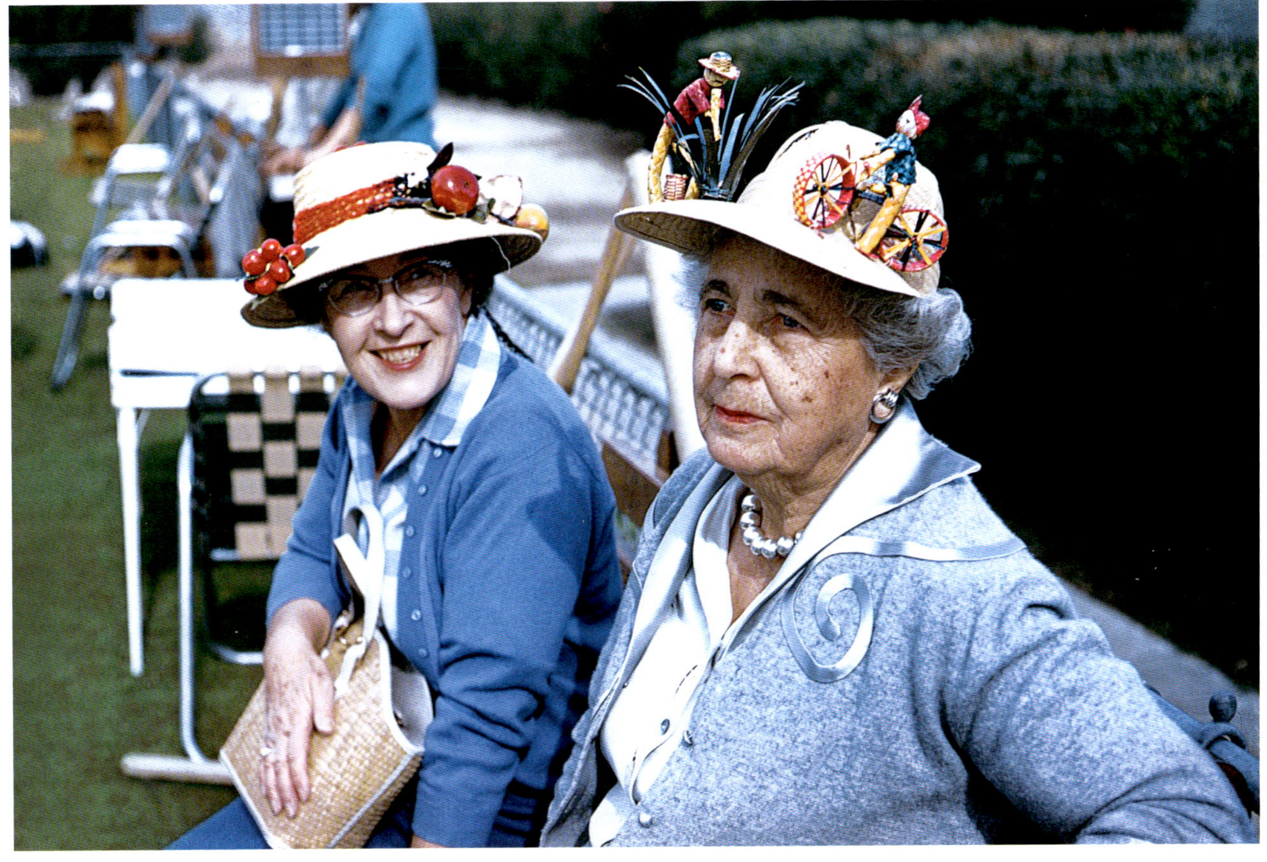

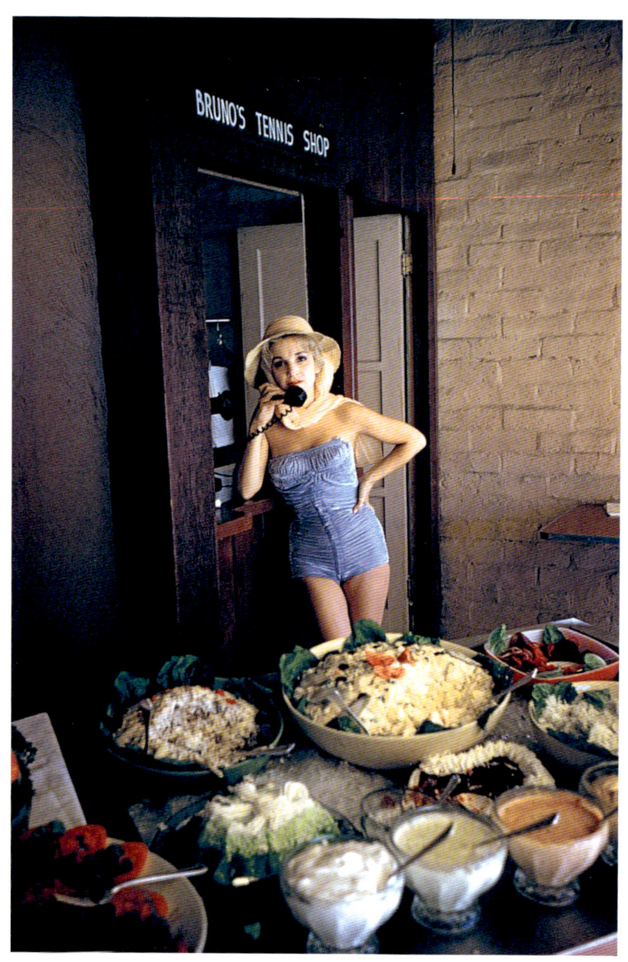
BRUNO'S TENNIS SHOP

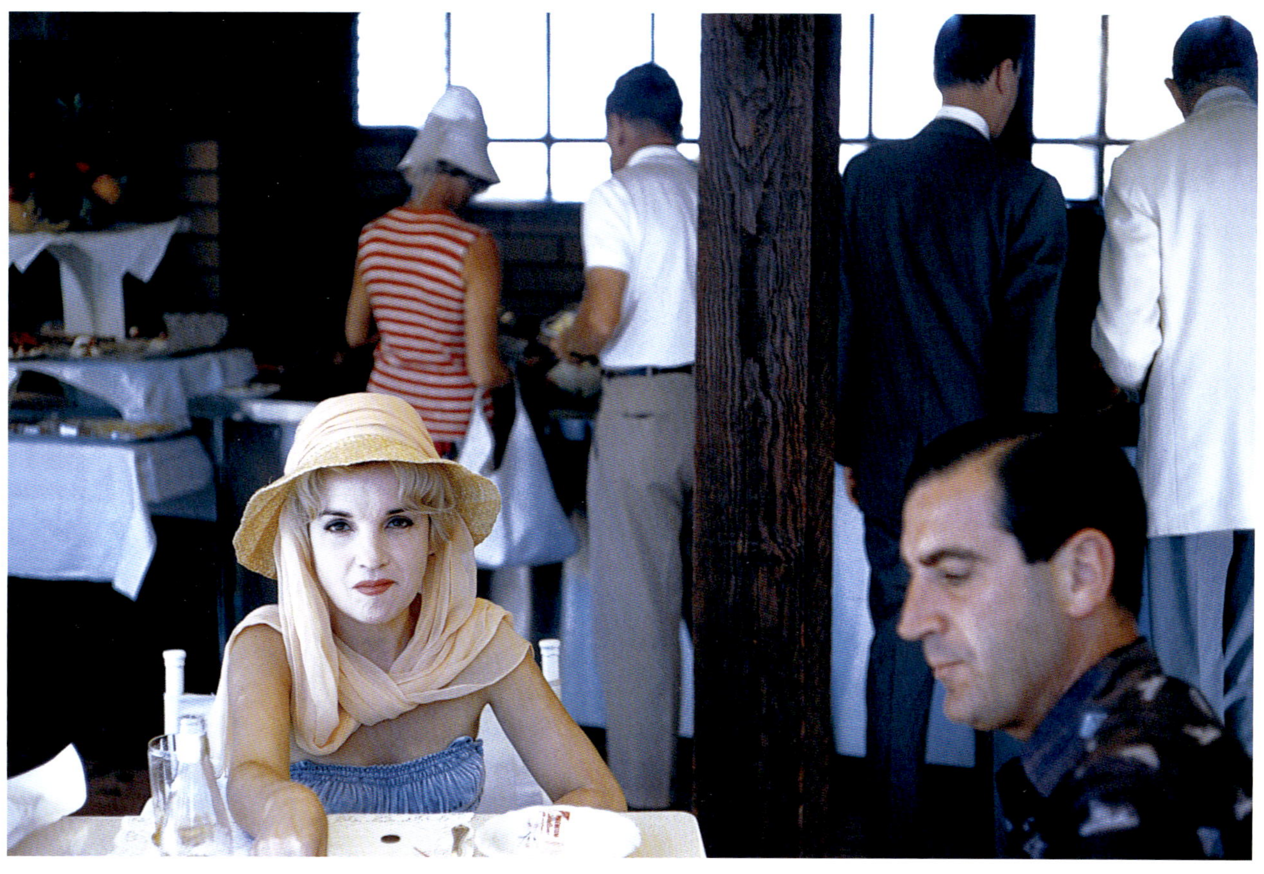

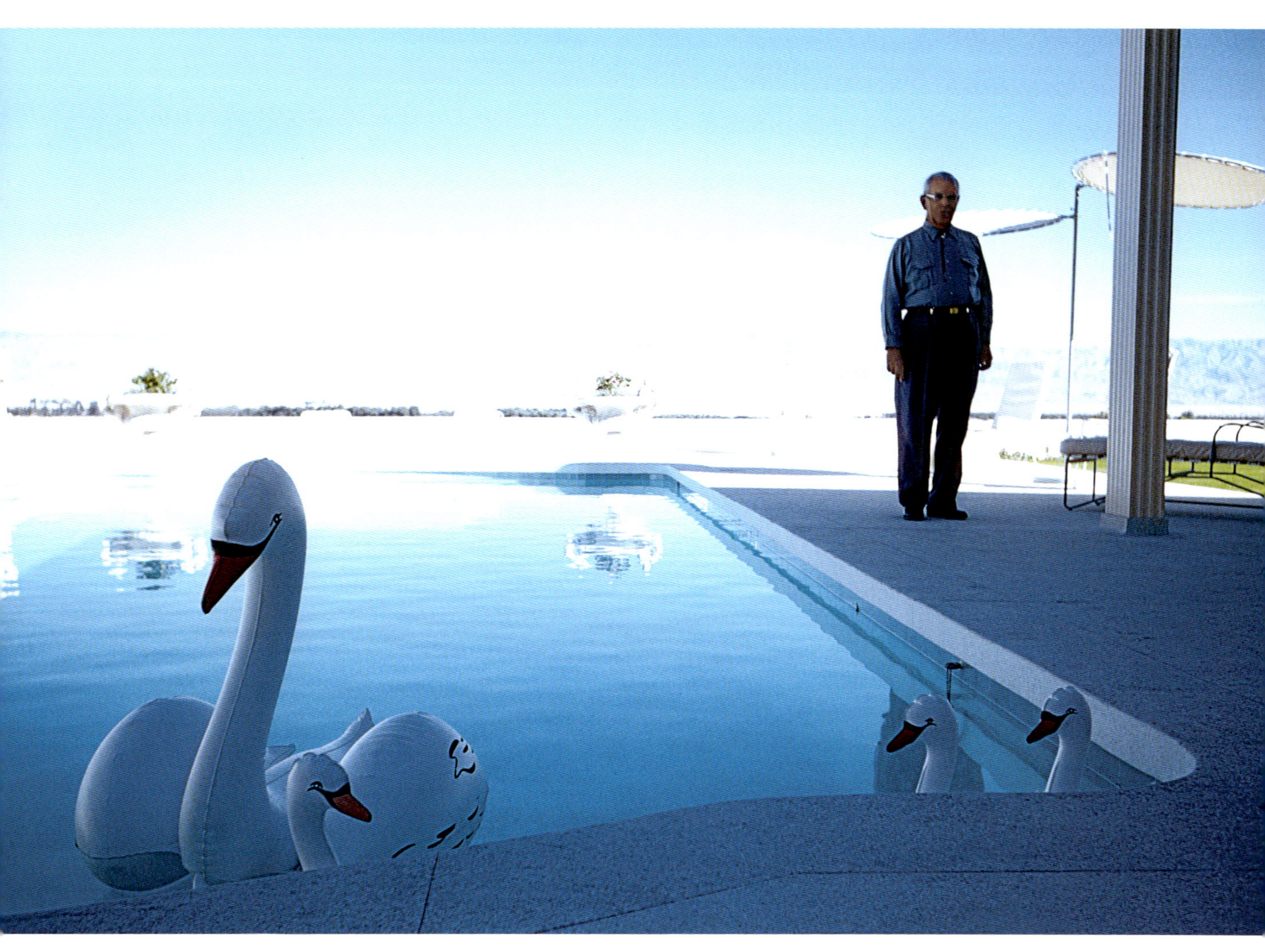

PALM SPRINGS 1960 • Robert Doisneau • 64

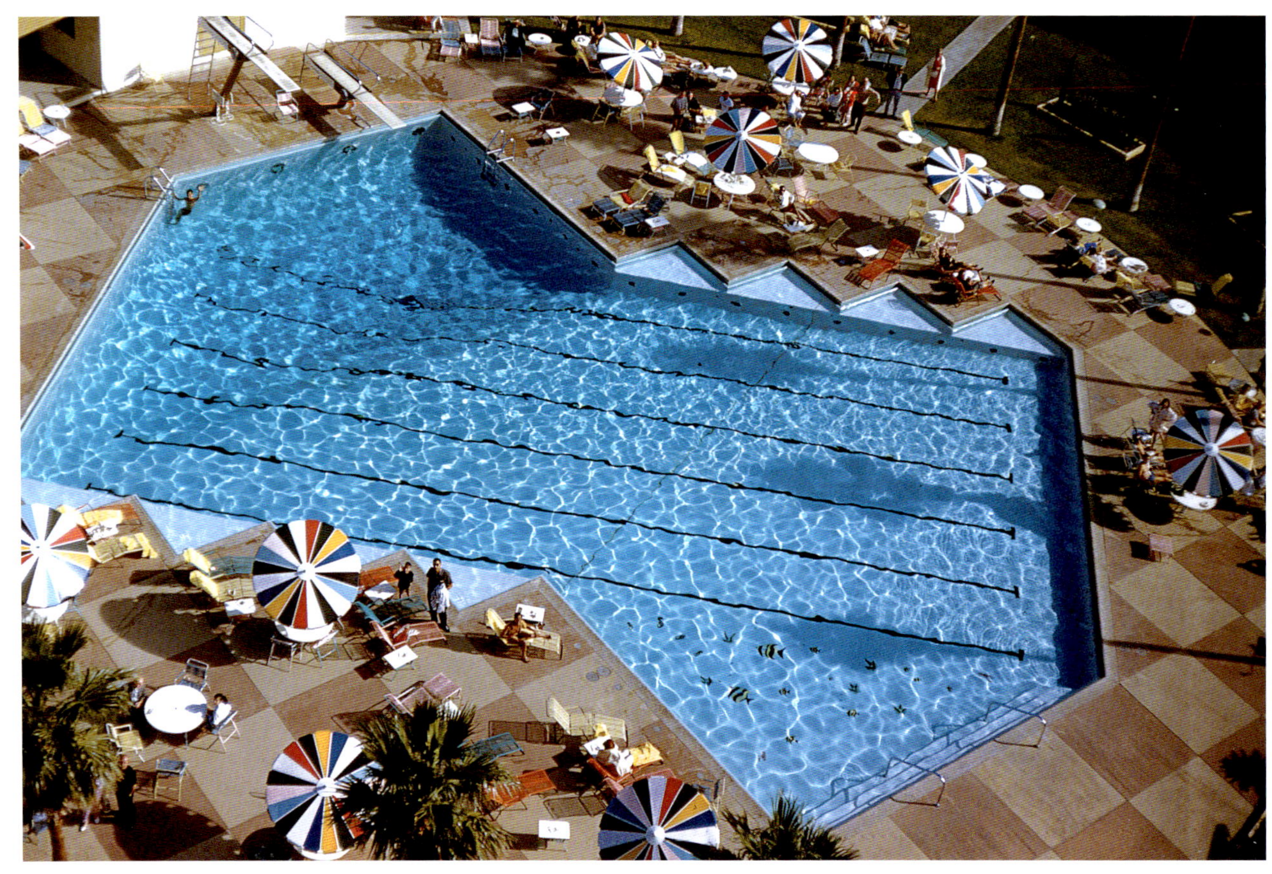

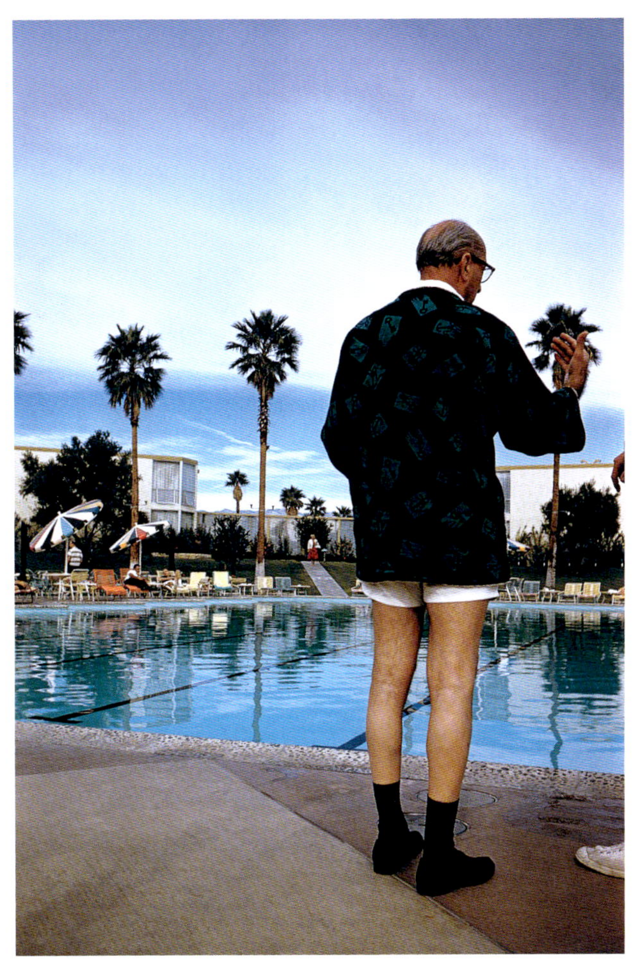

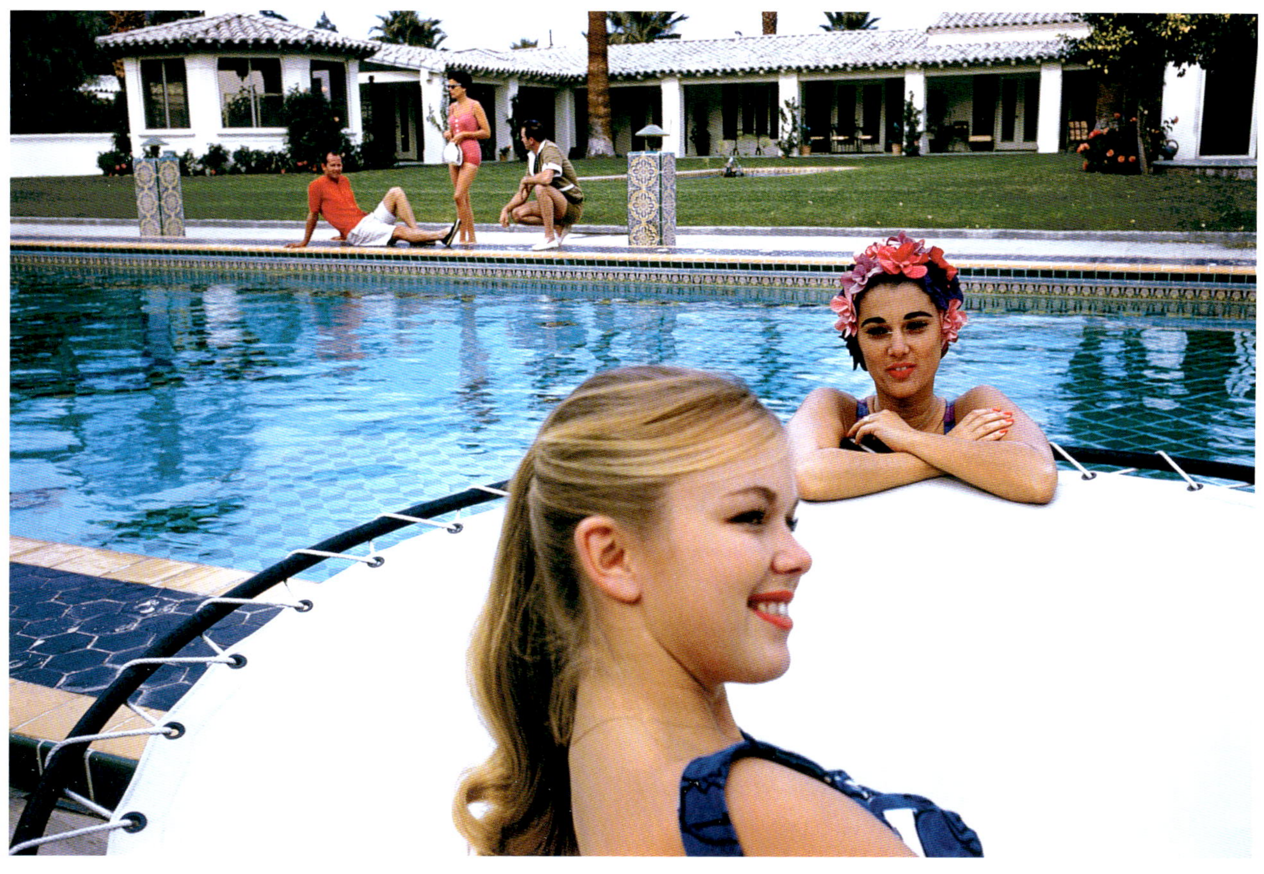

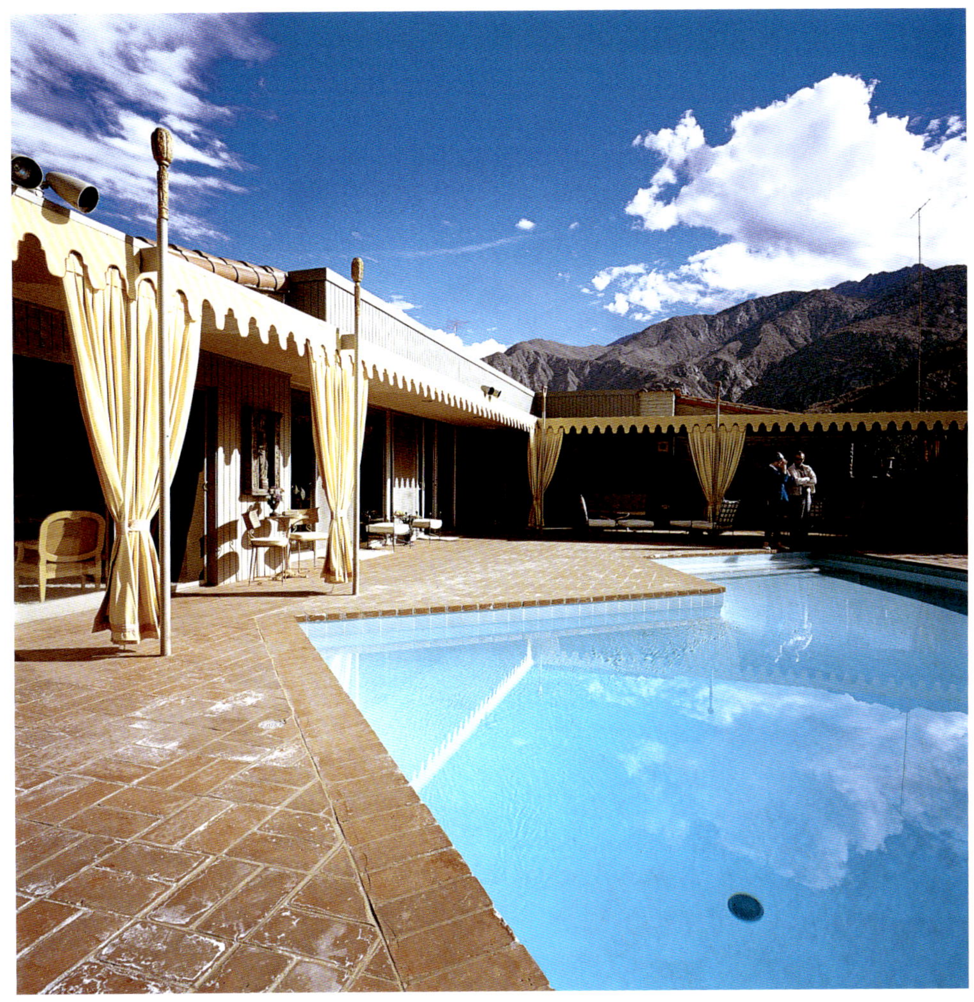

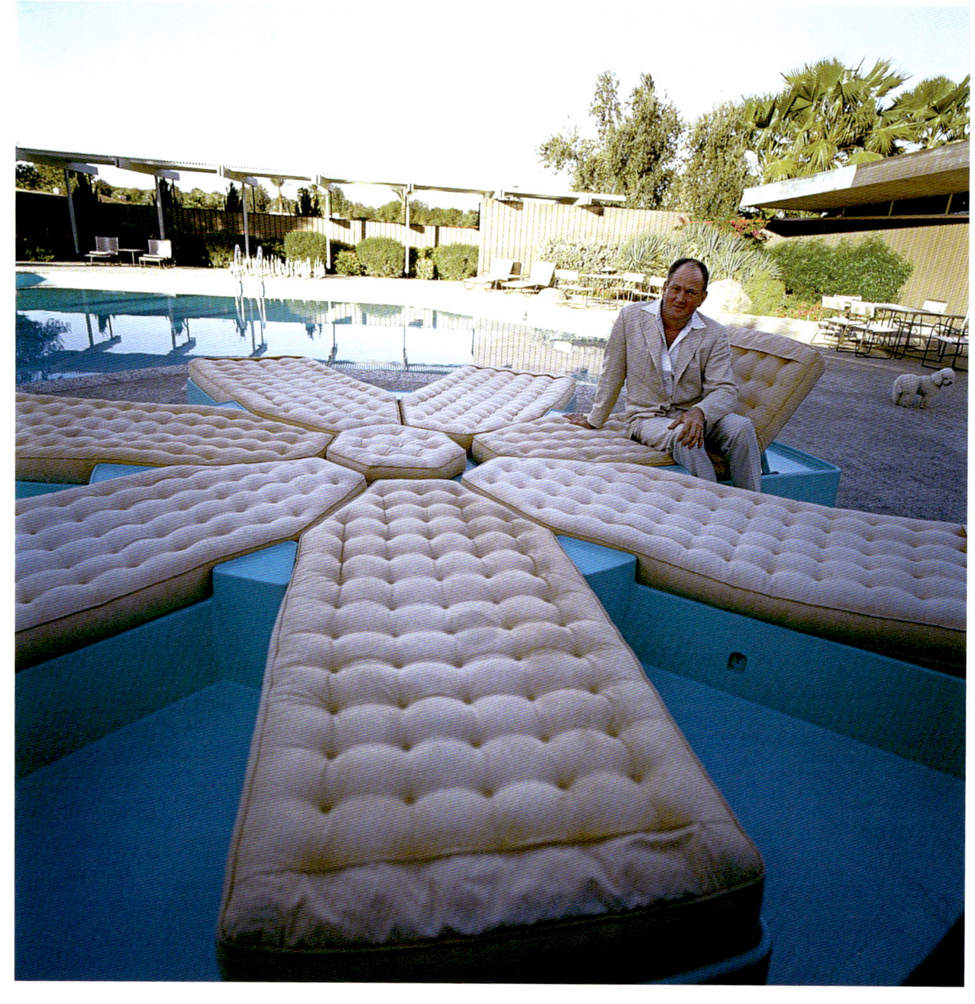

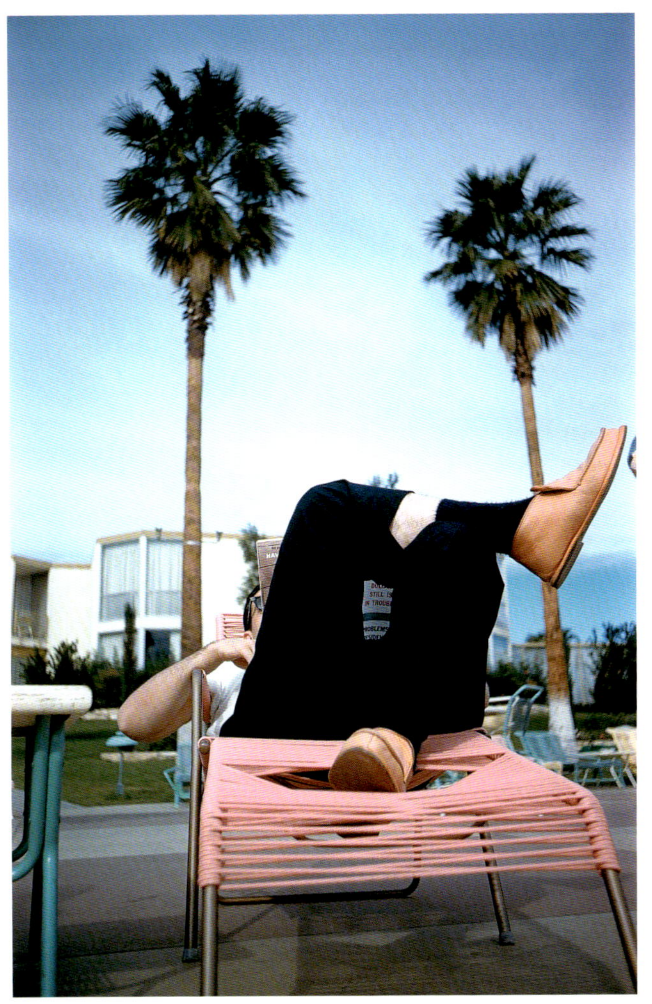

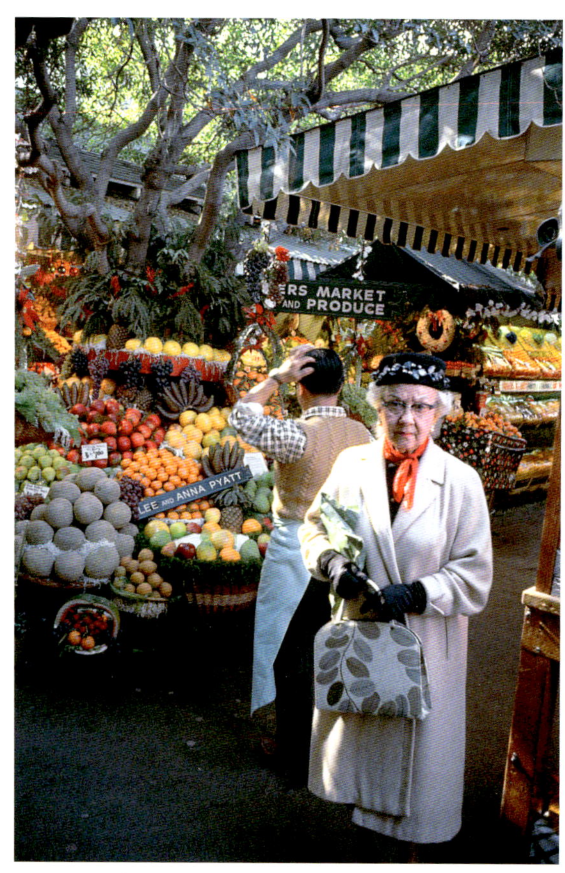
ERS MARKET
AND PRODUCE
LEE AND ANNA PYATT

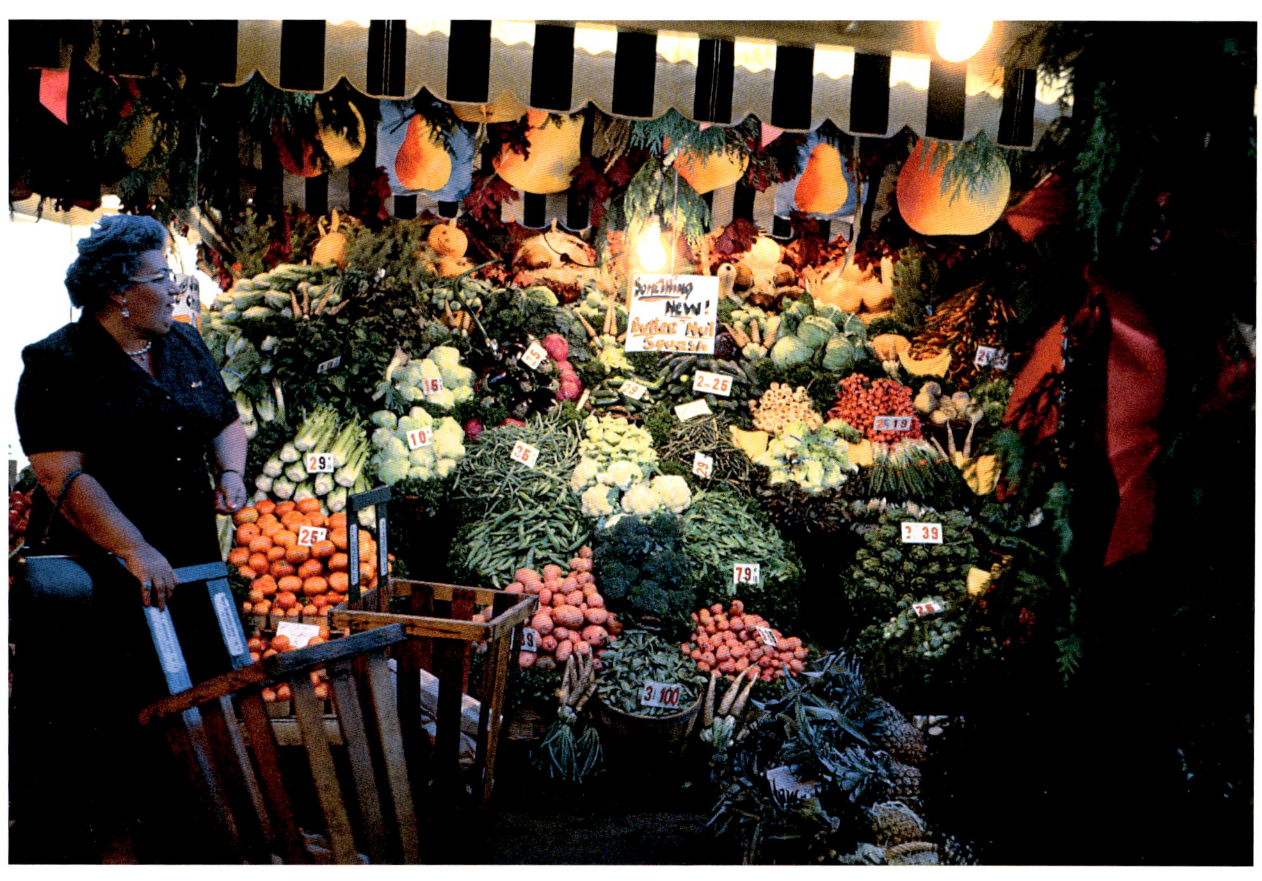
Something
NEW!
Butter Nut
Squash

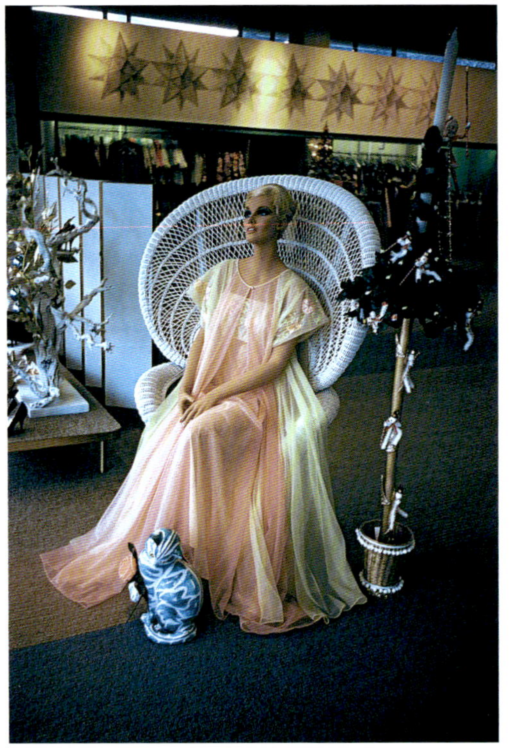

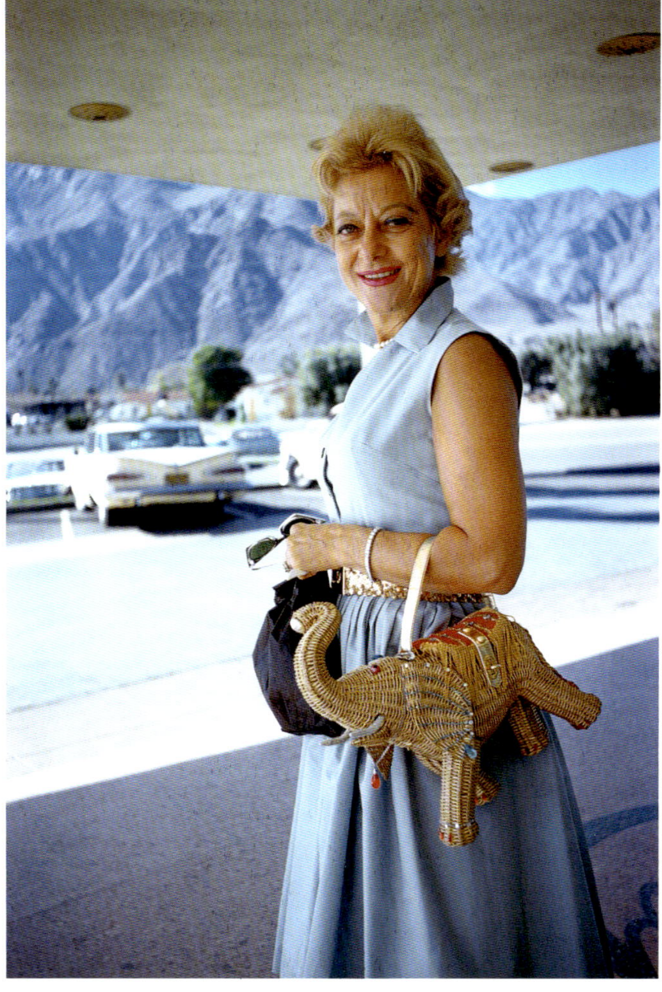

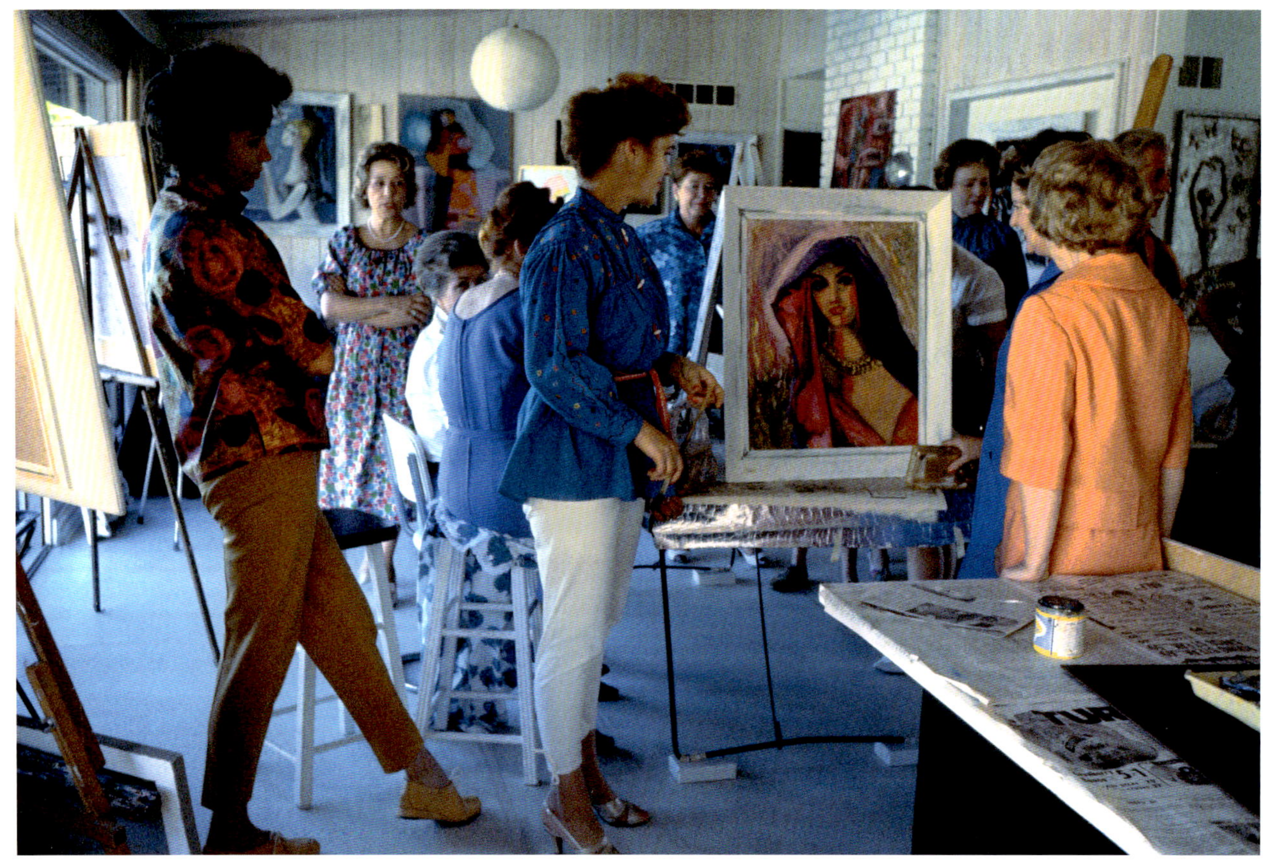

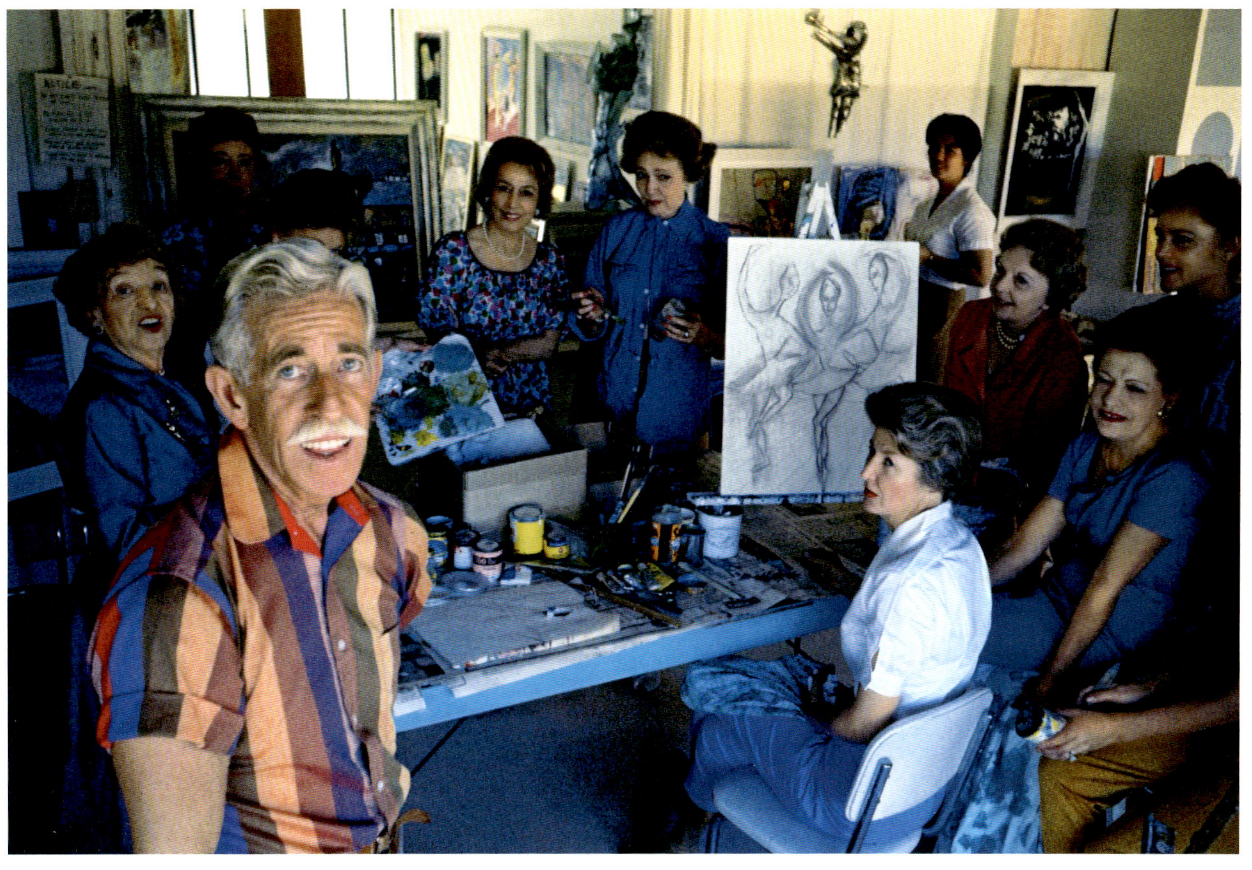

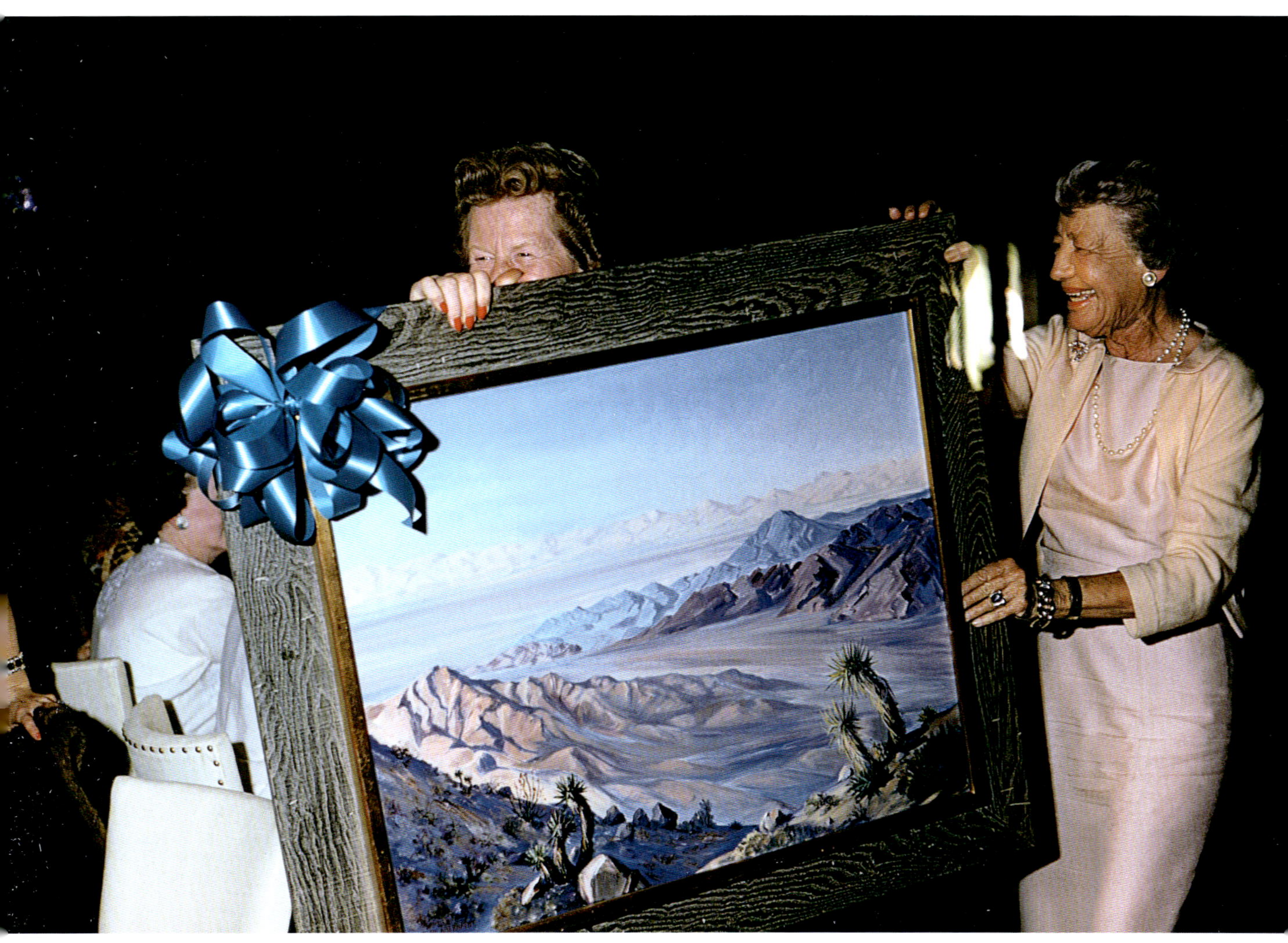

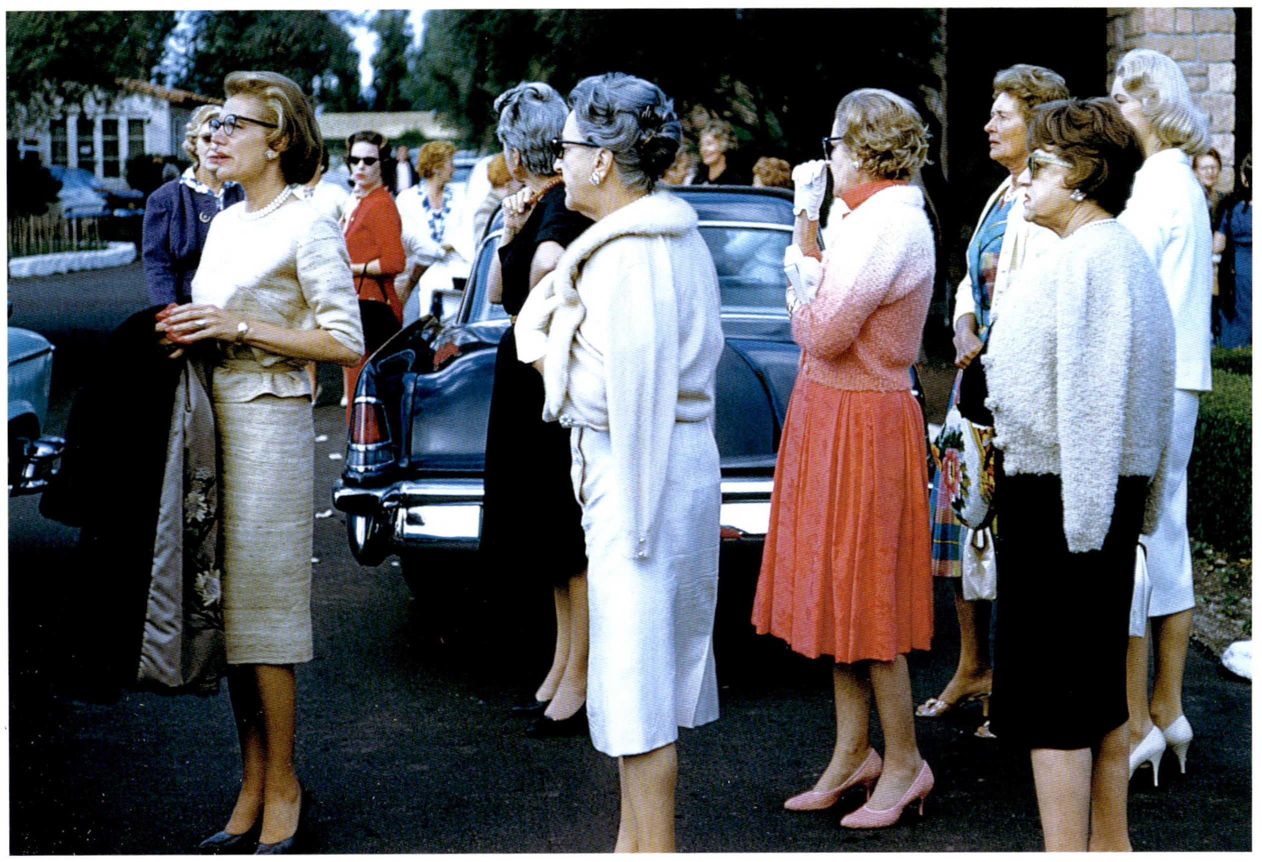

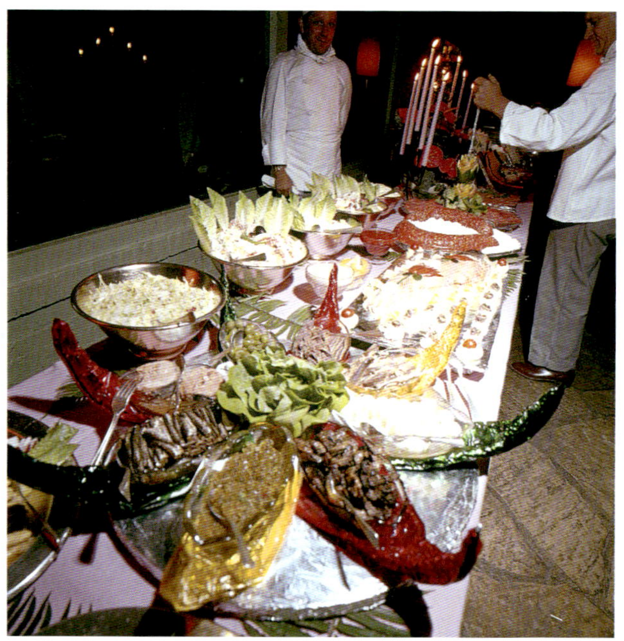

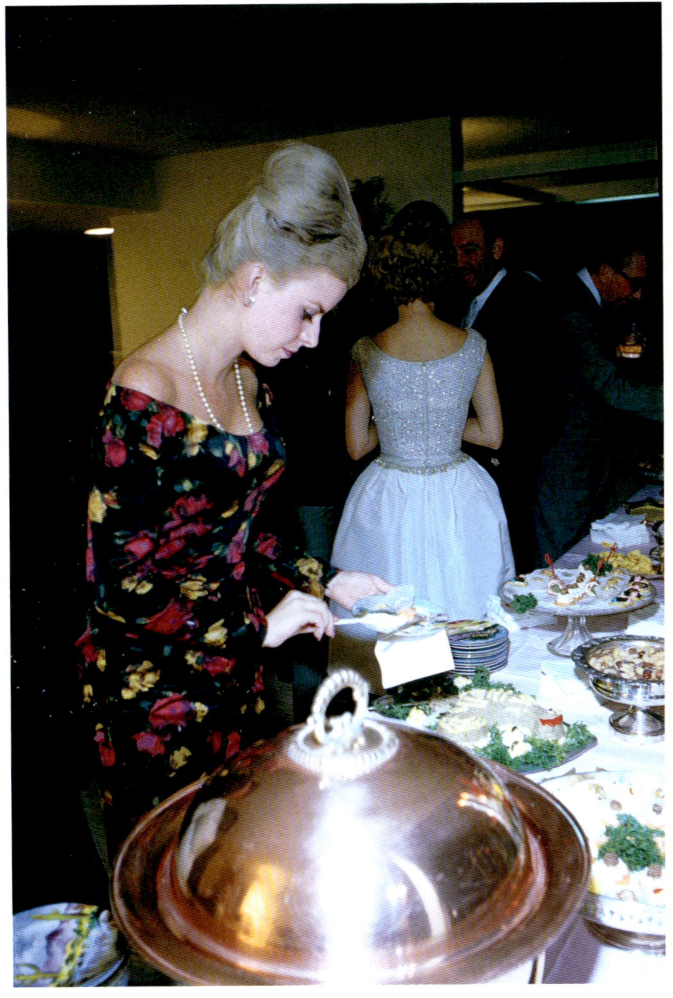

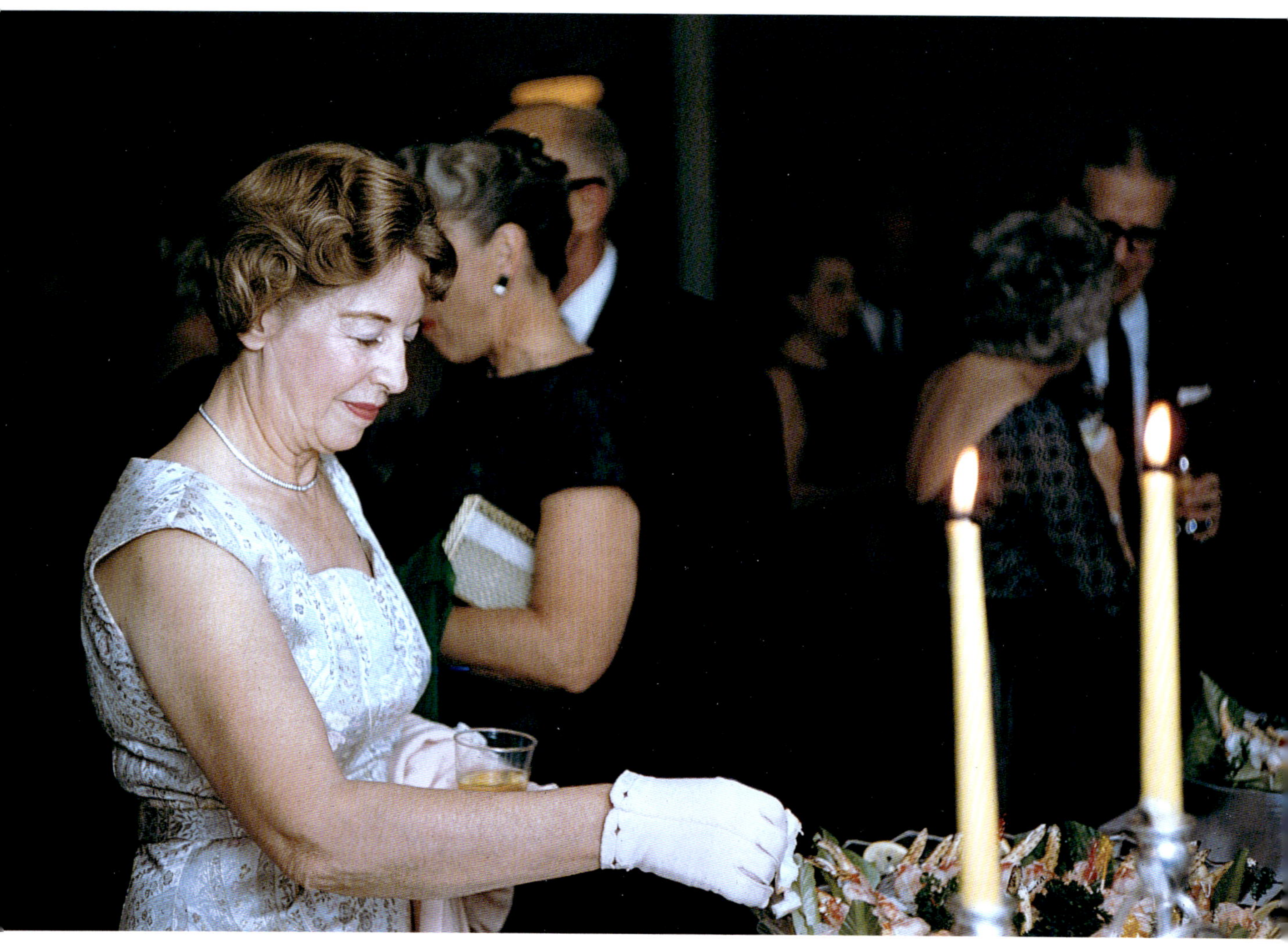

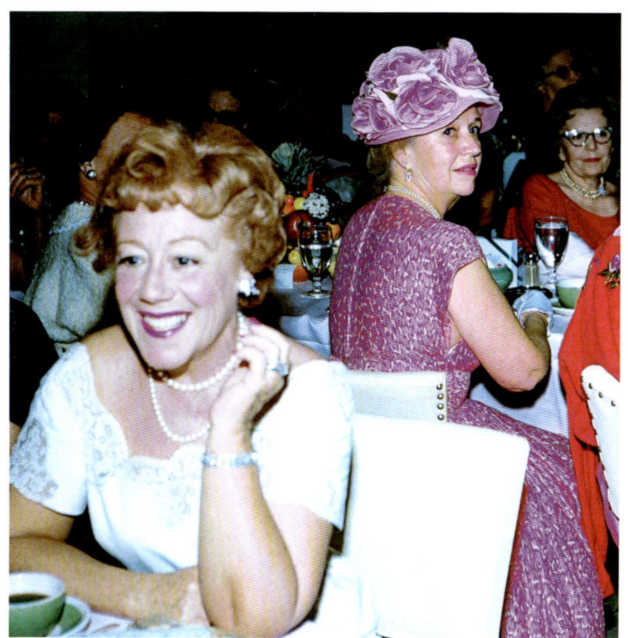

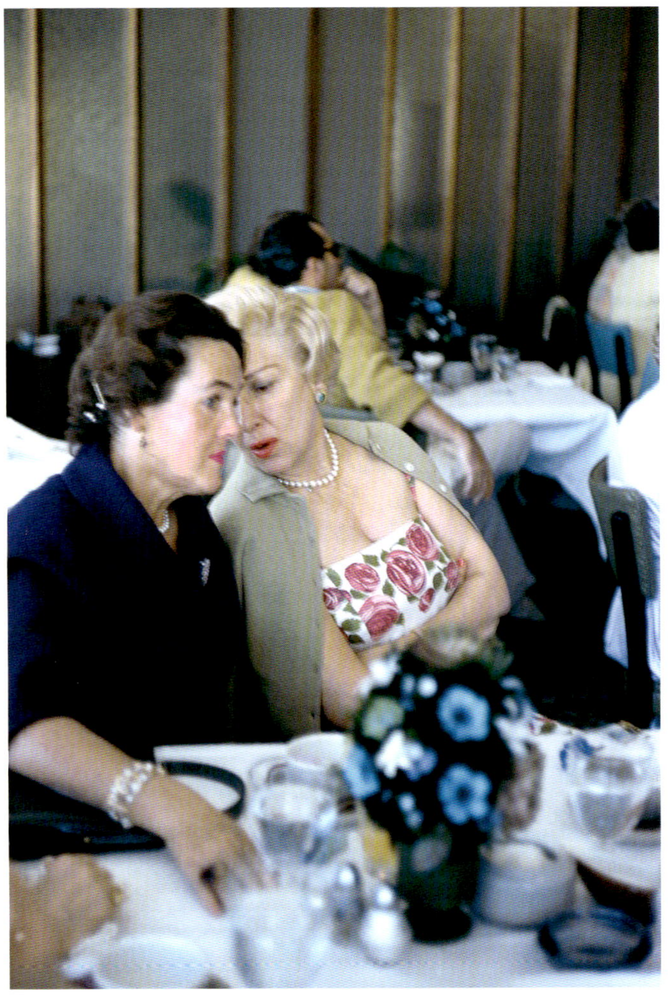

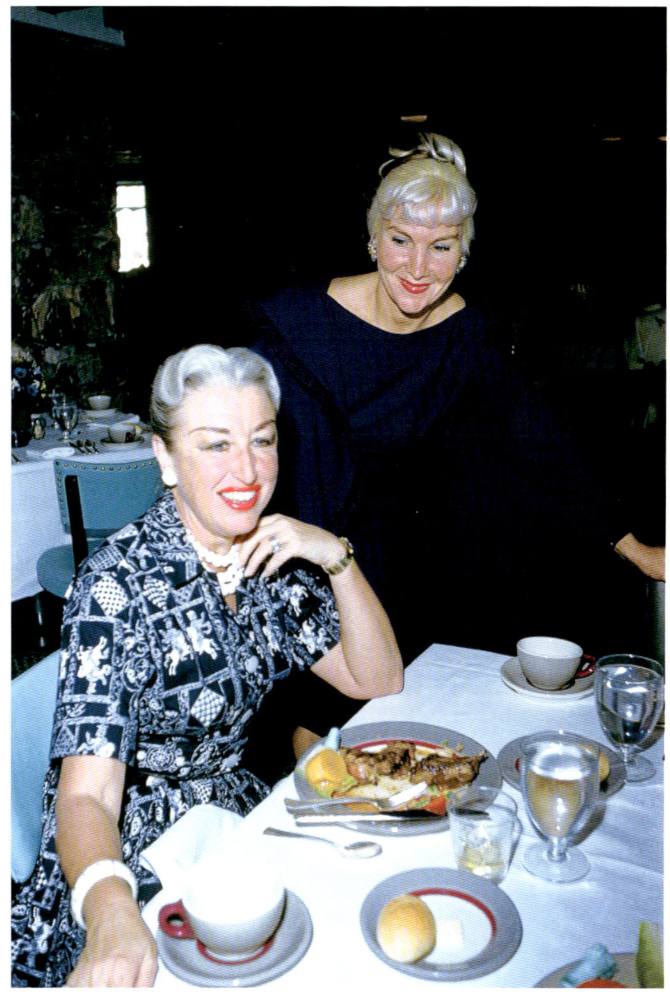

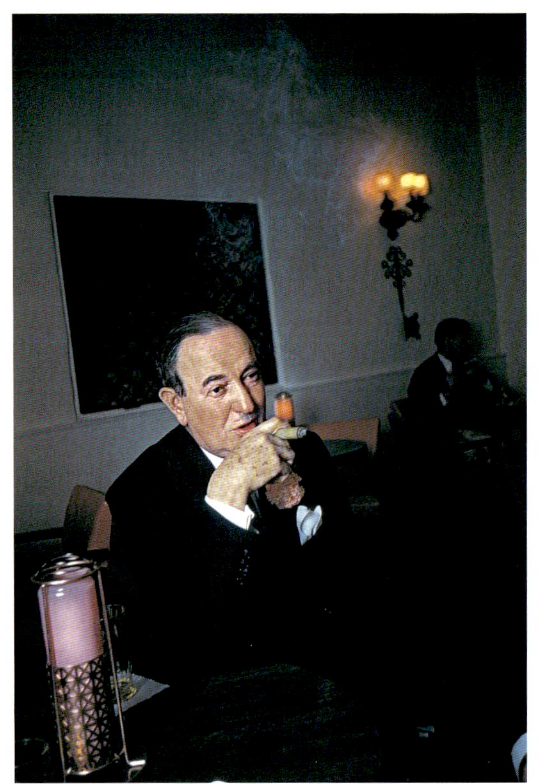

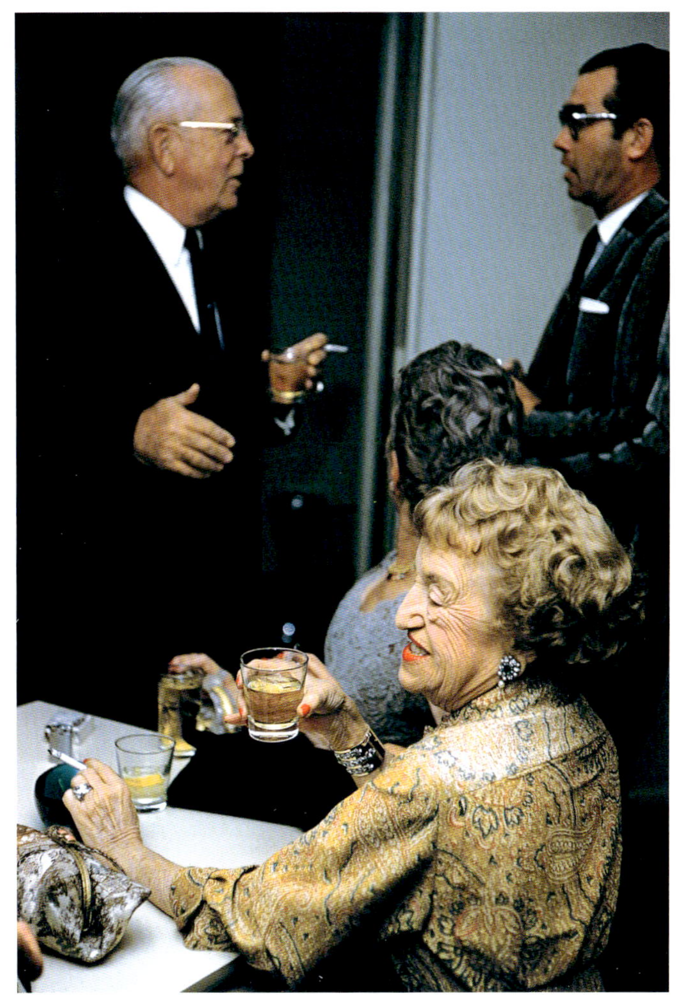

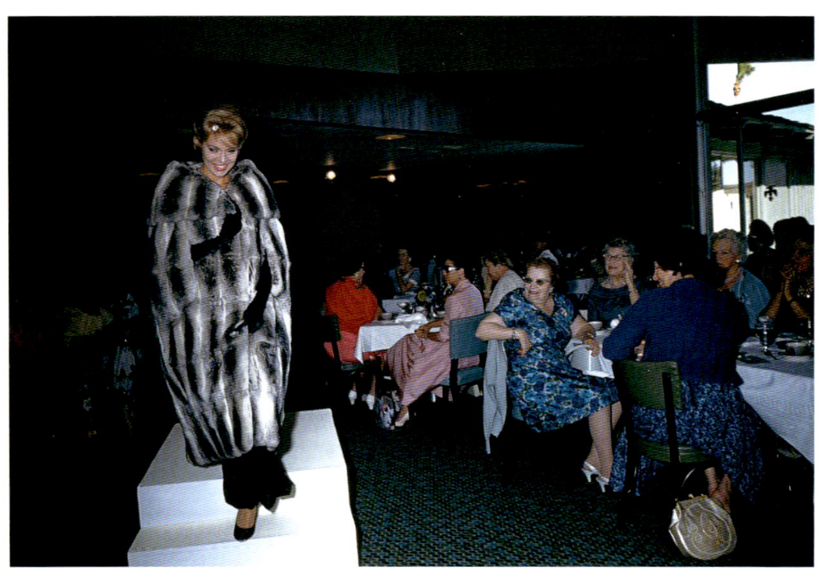

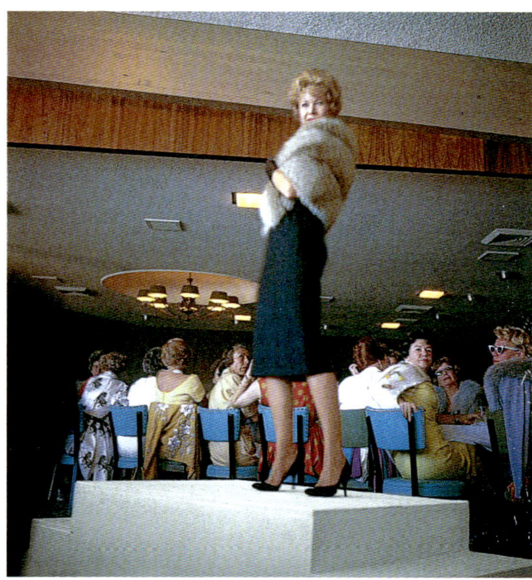

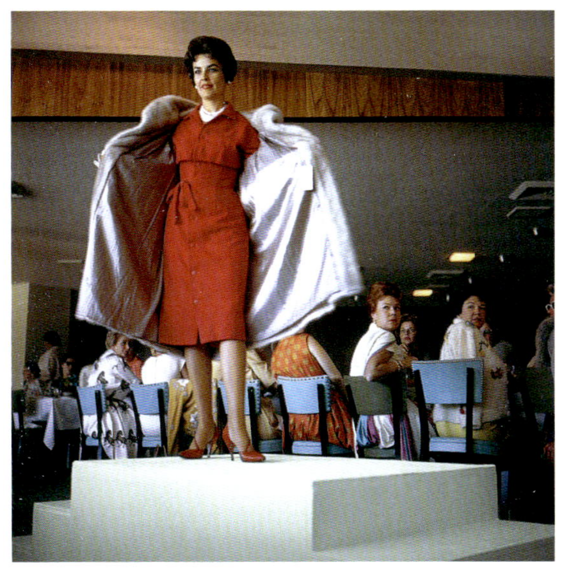

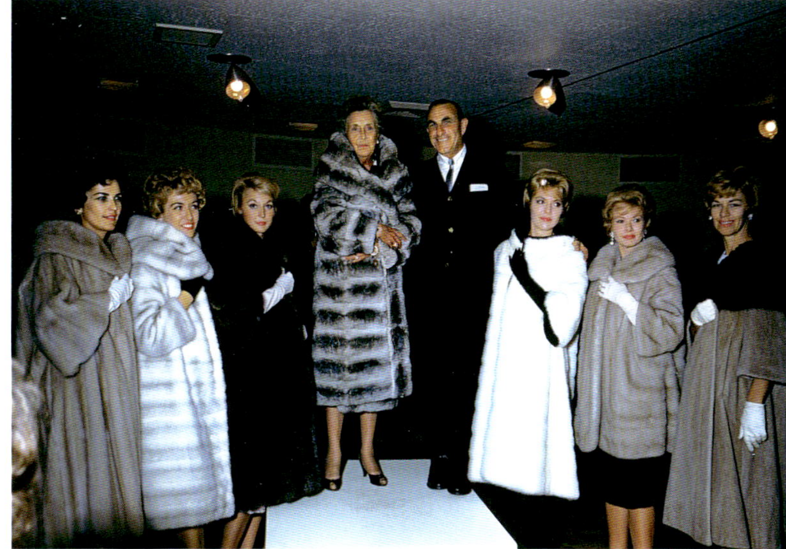

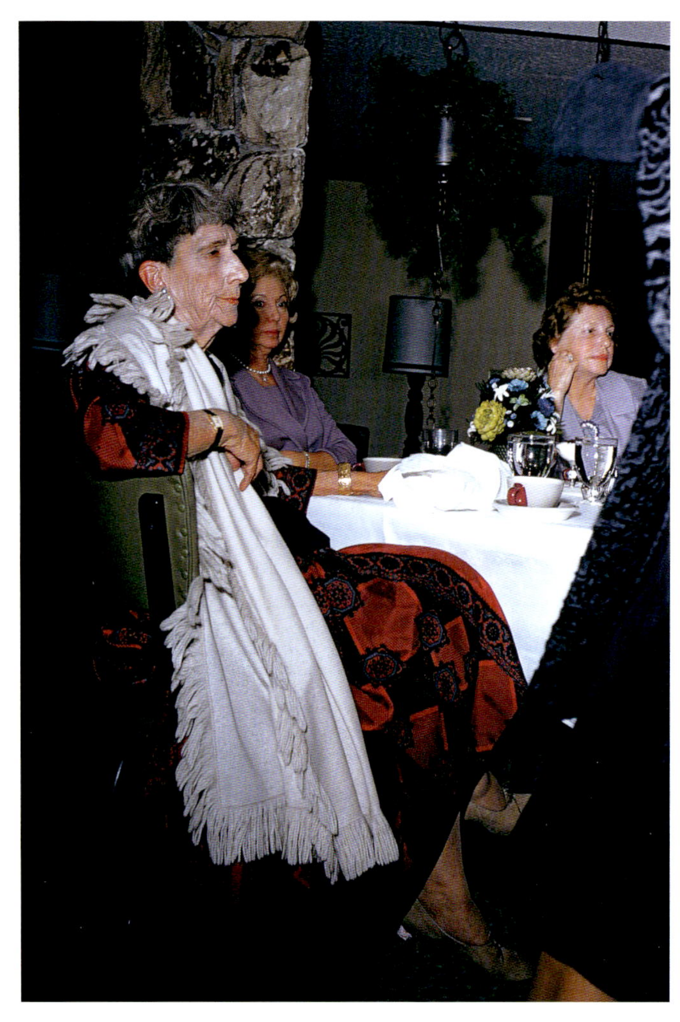

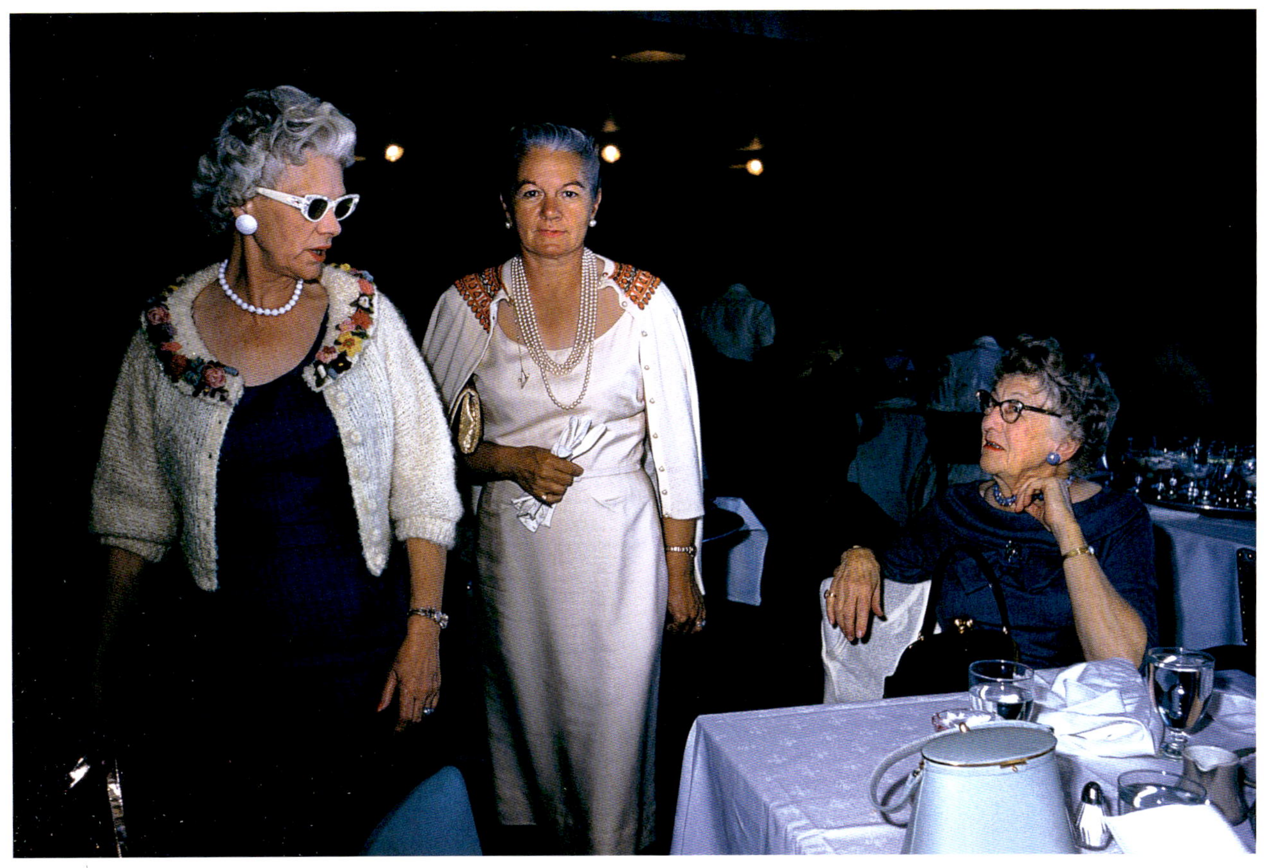

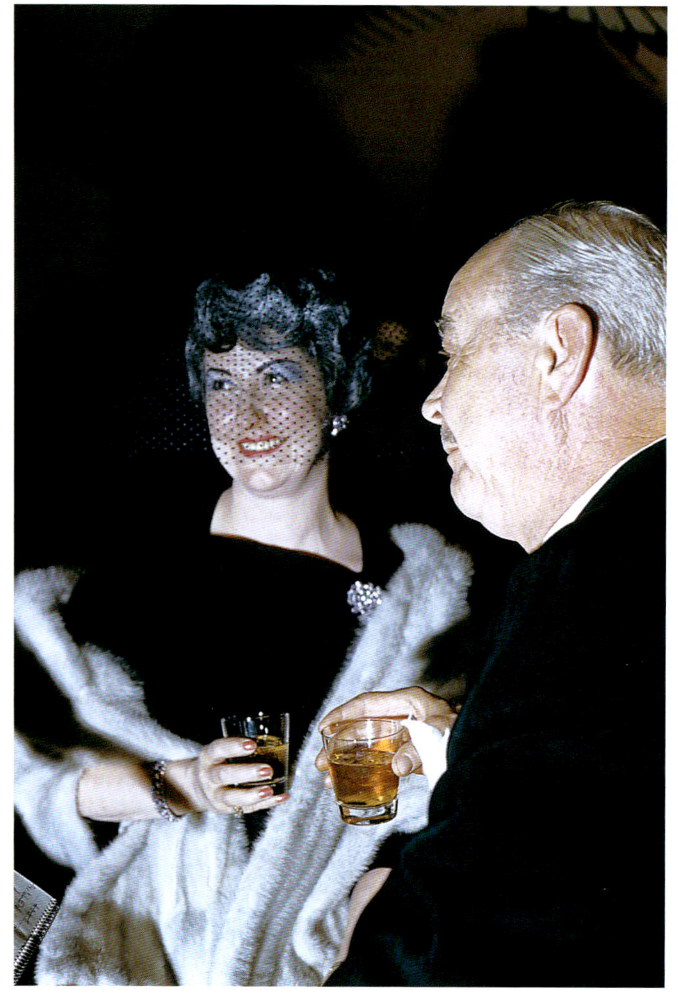

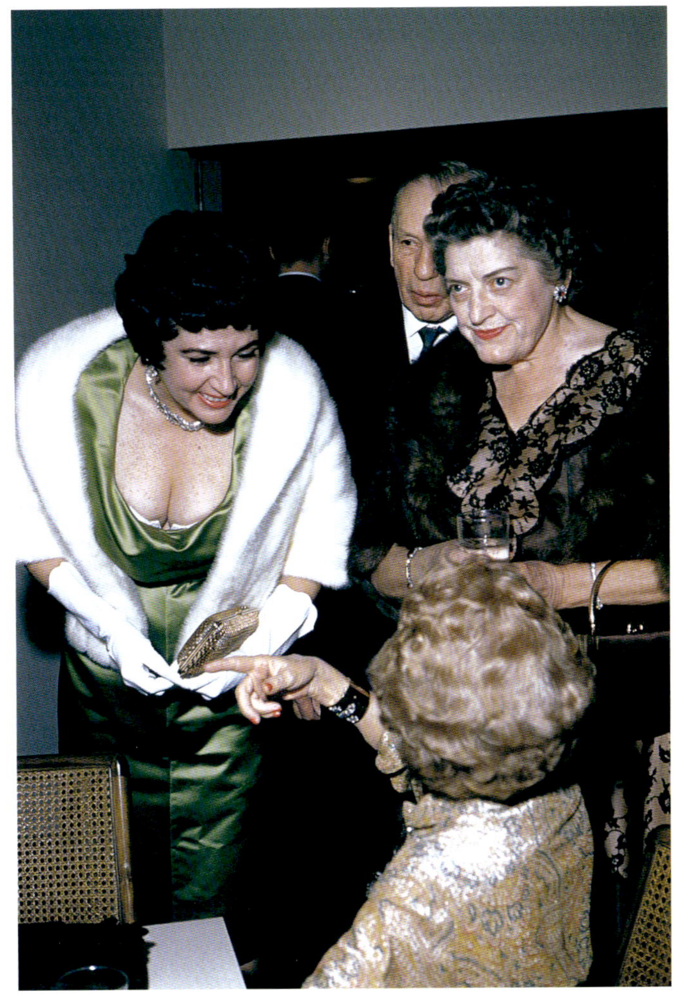

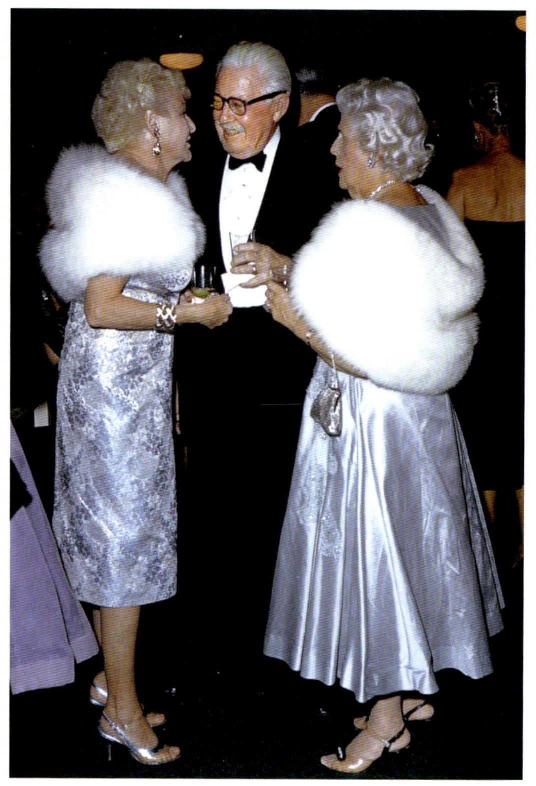

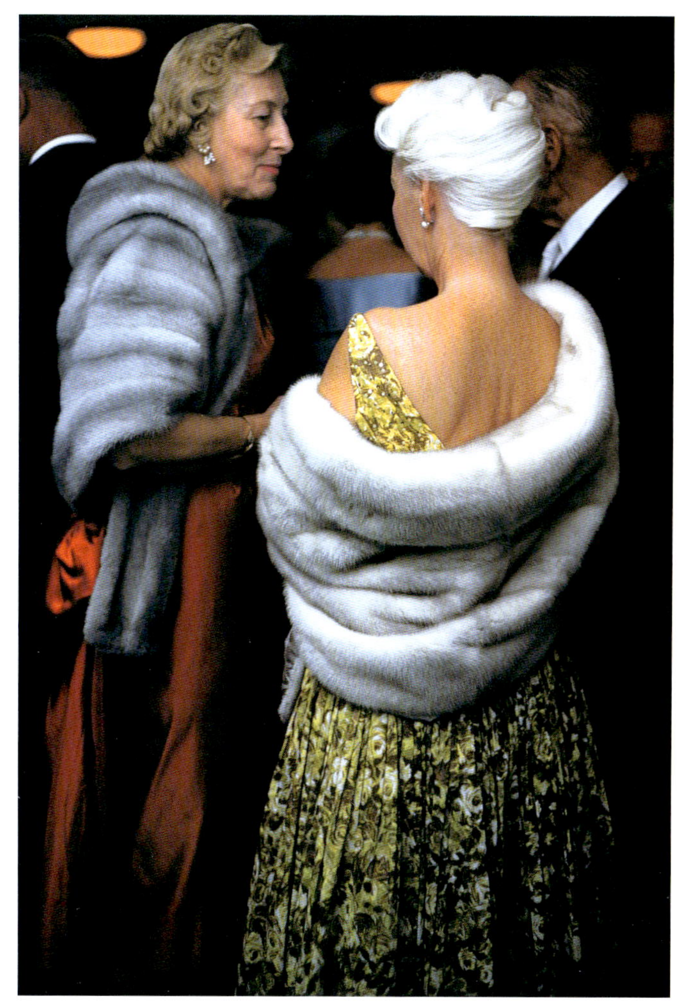

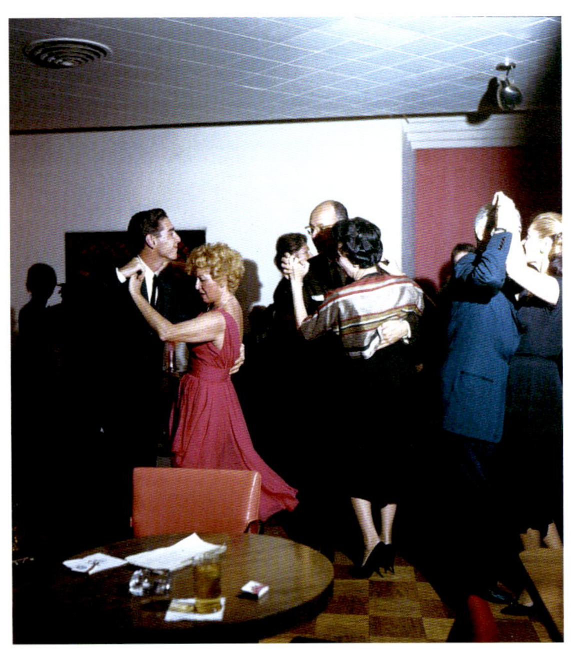

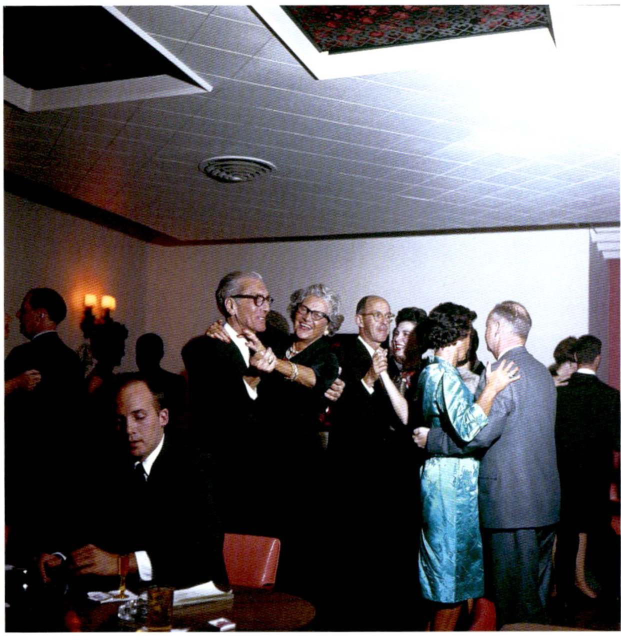

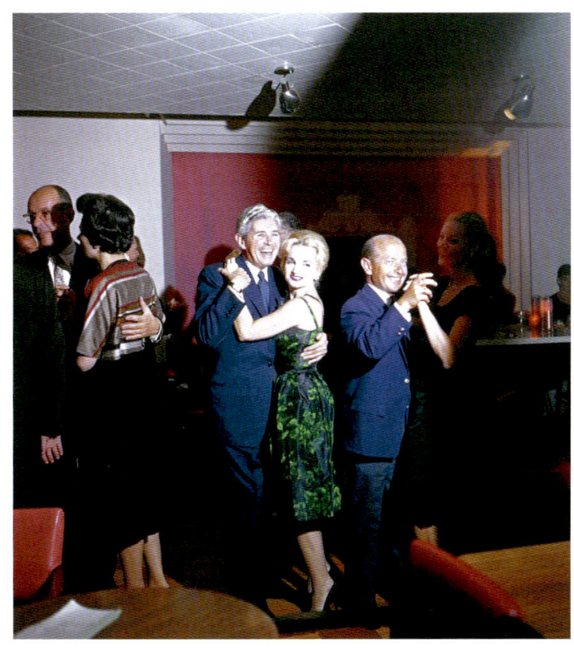

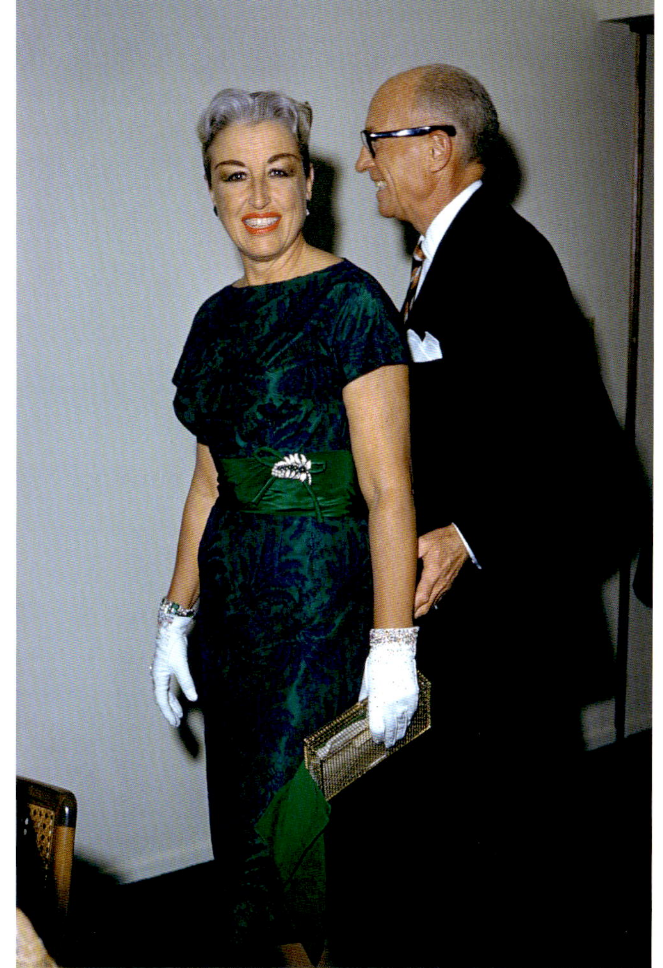

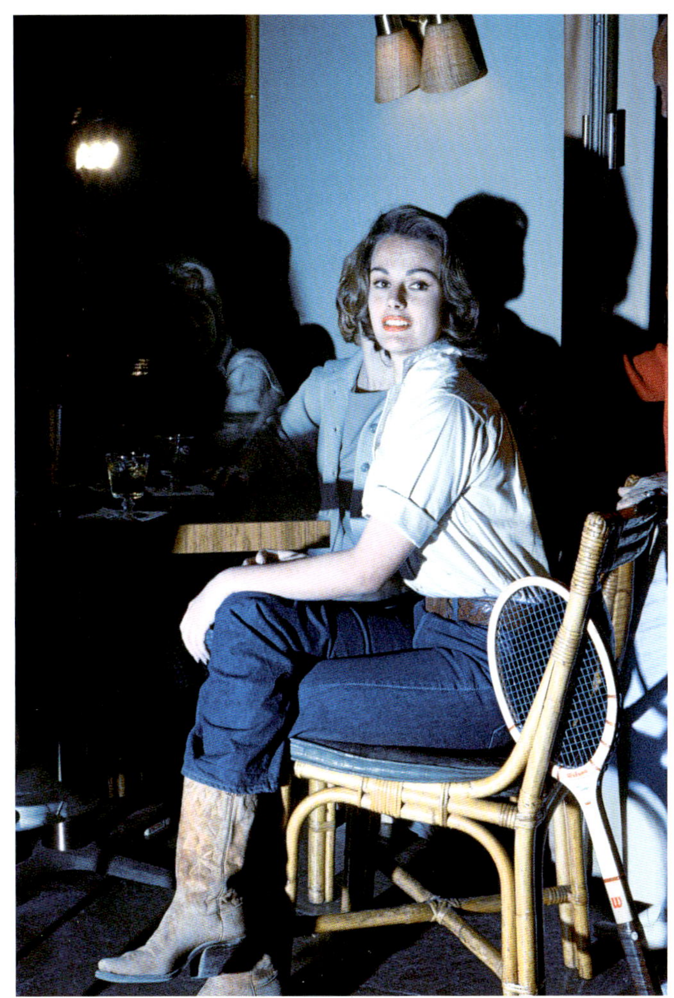

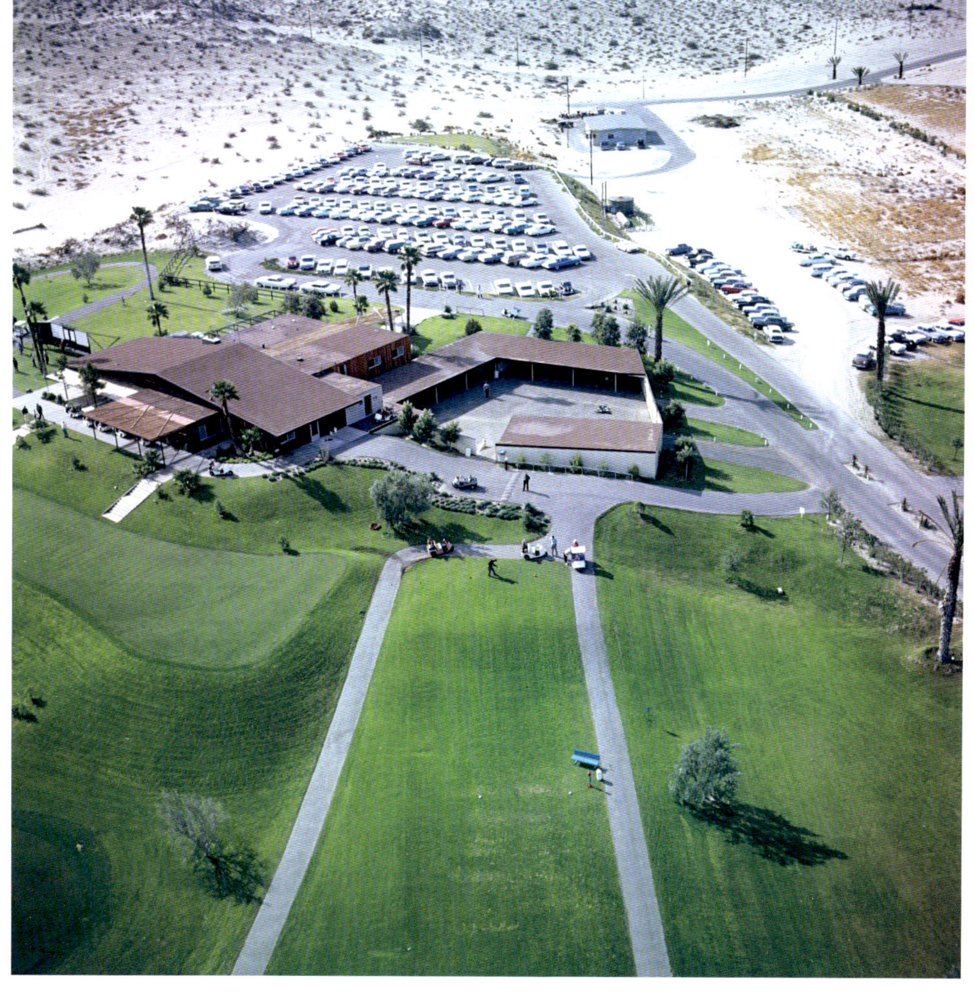

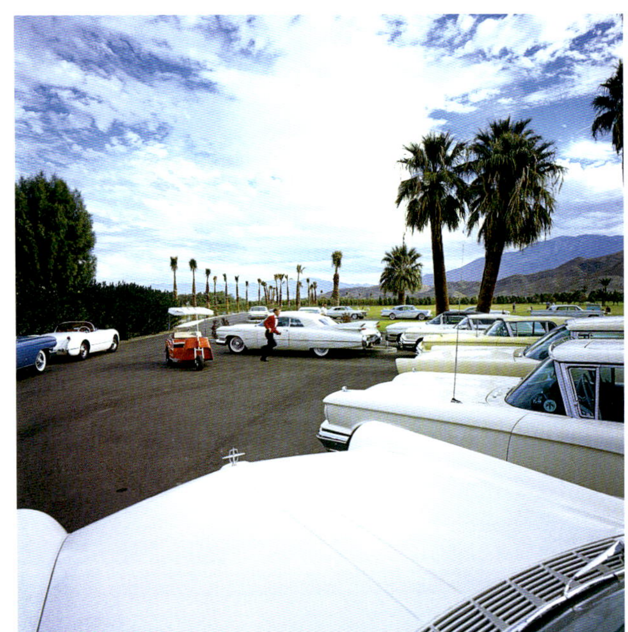

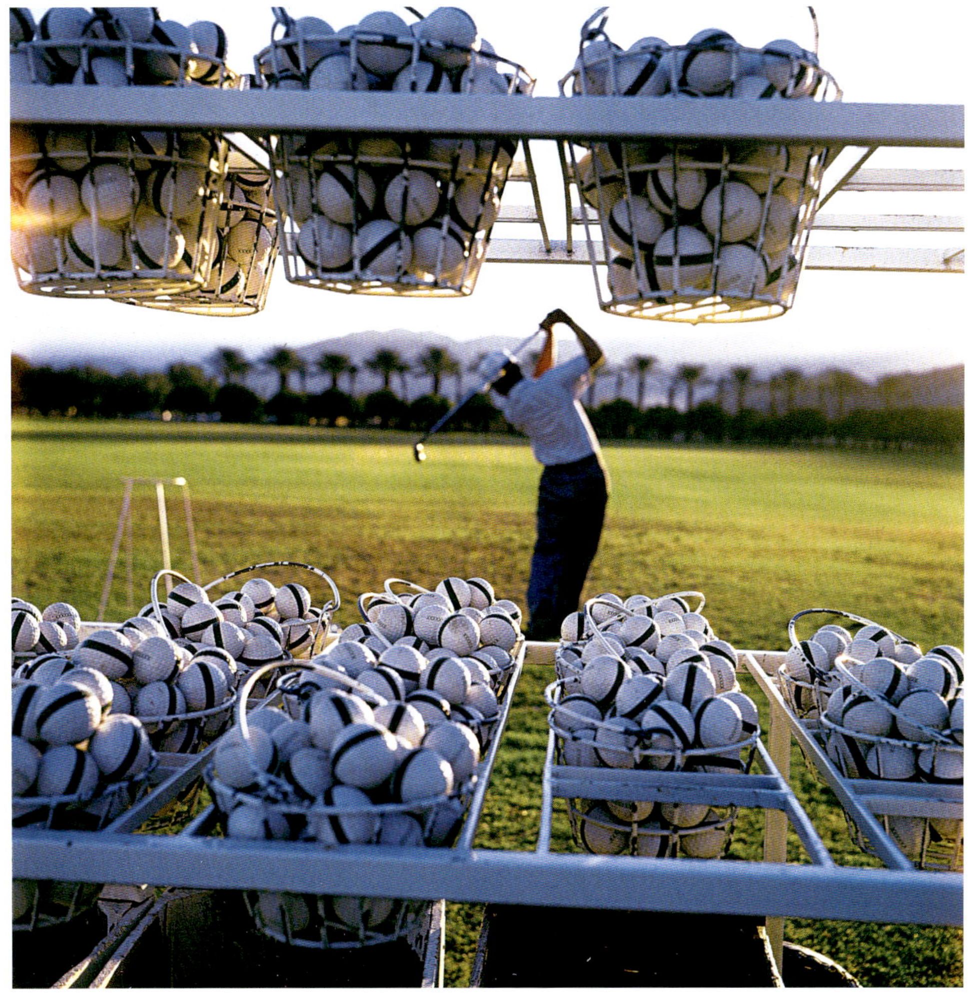

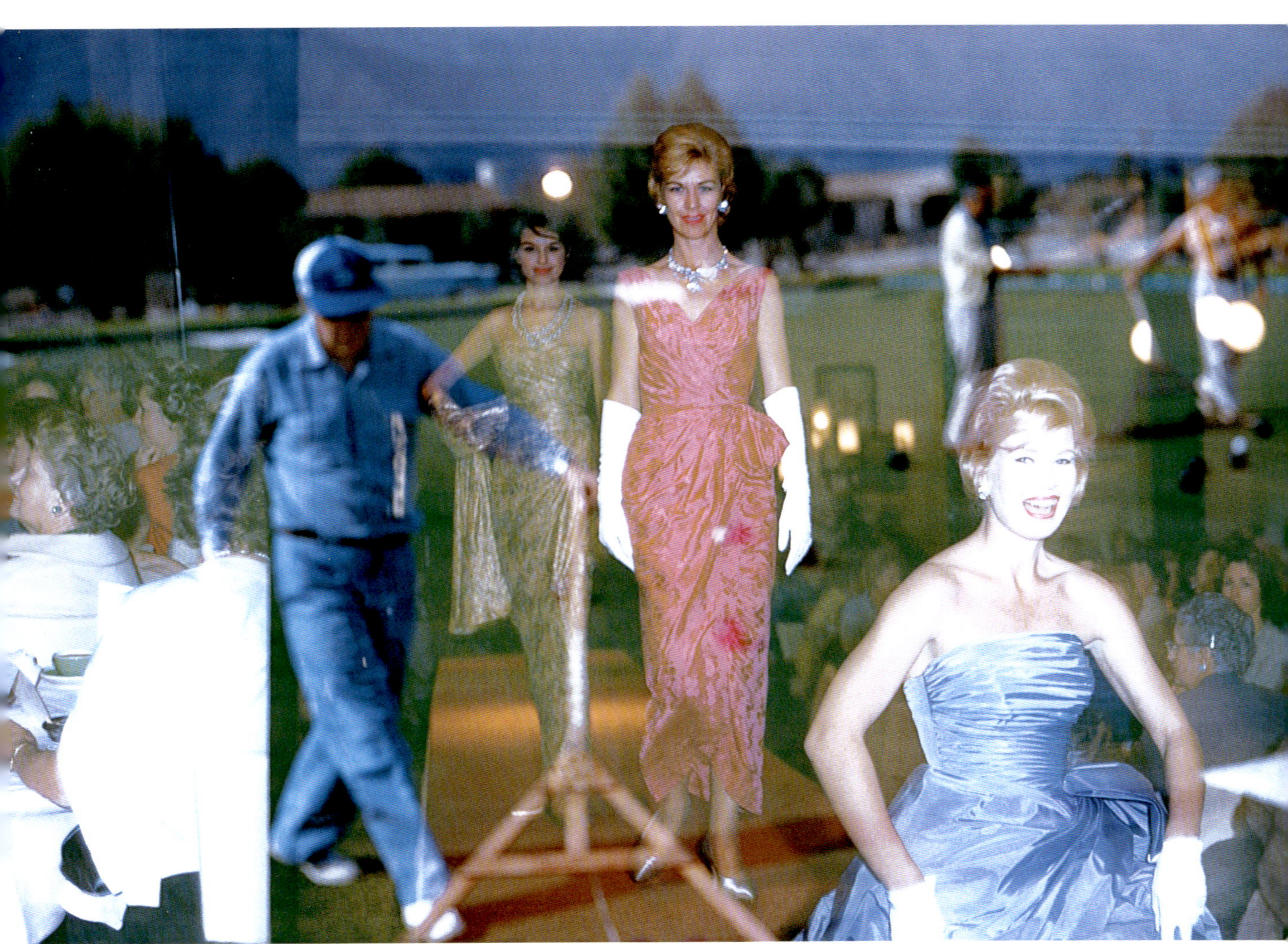

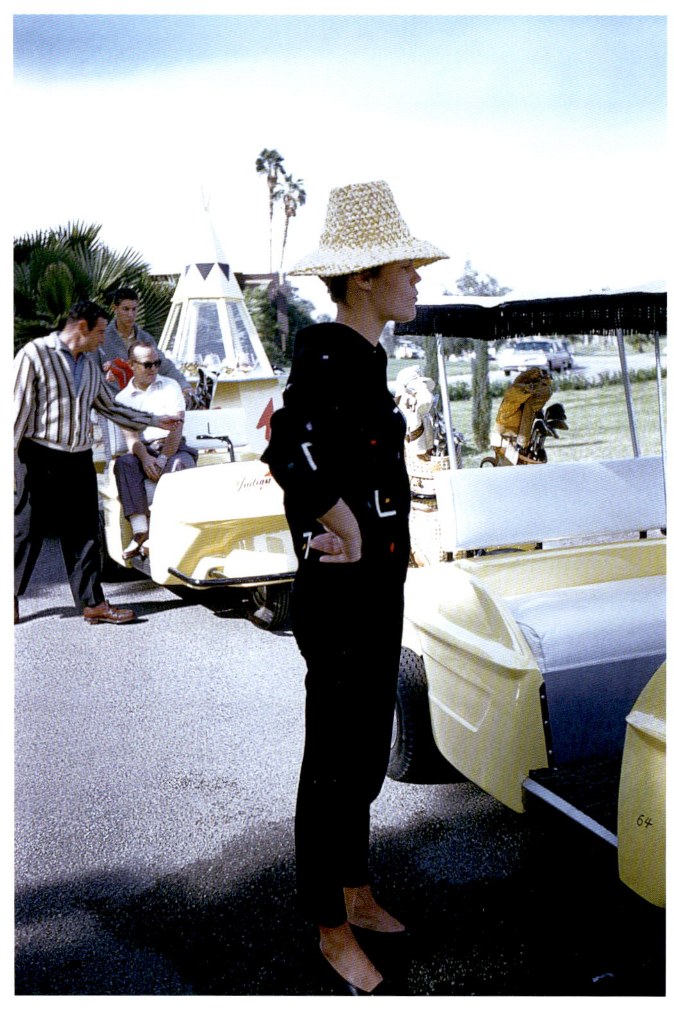

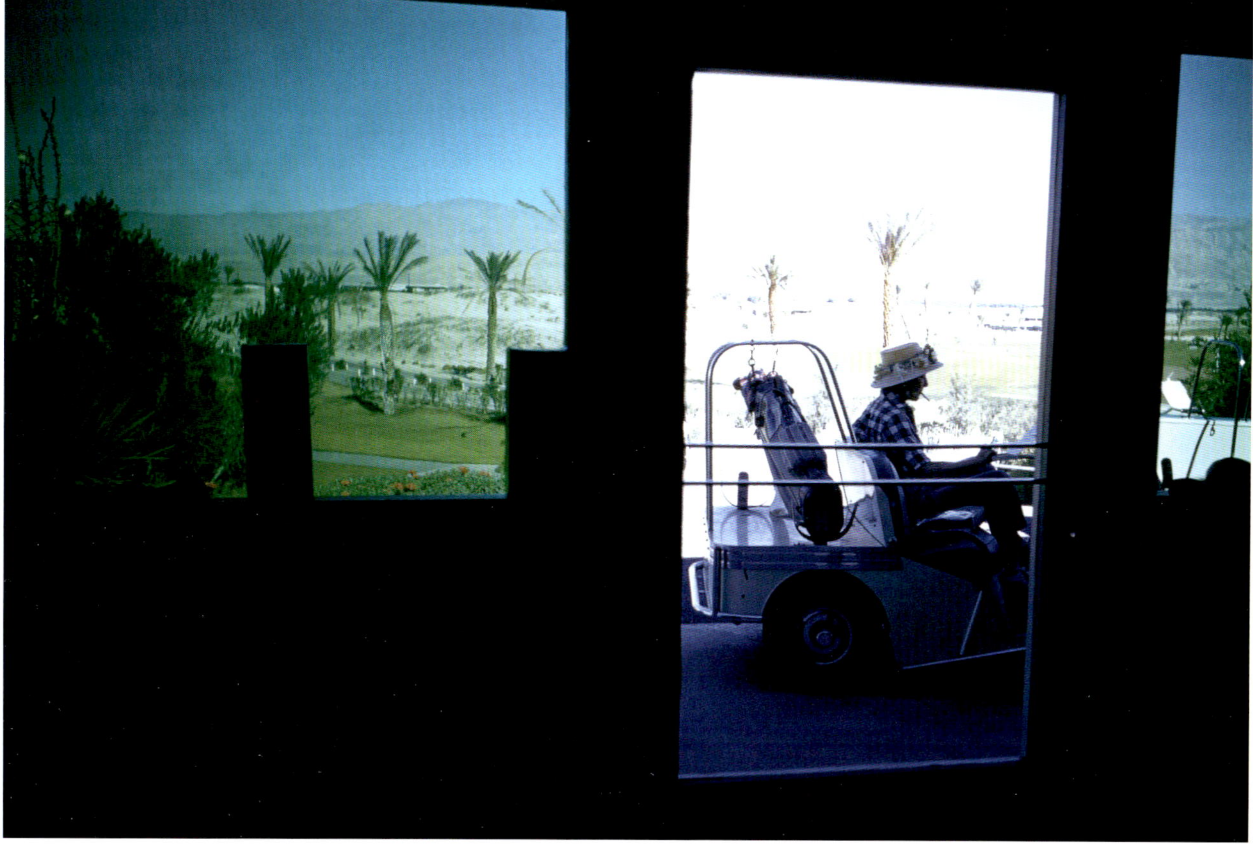

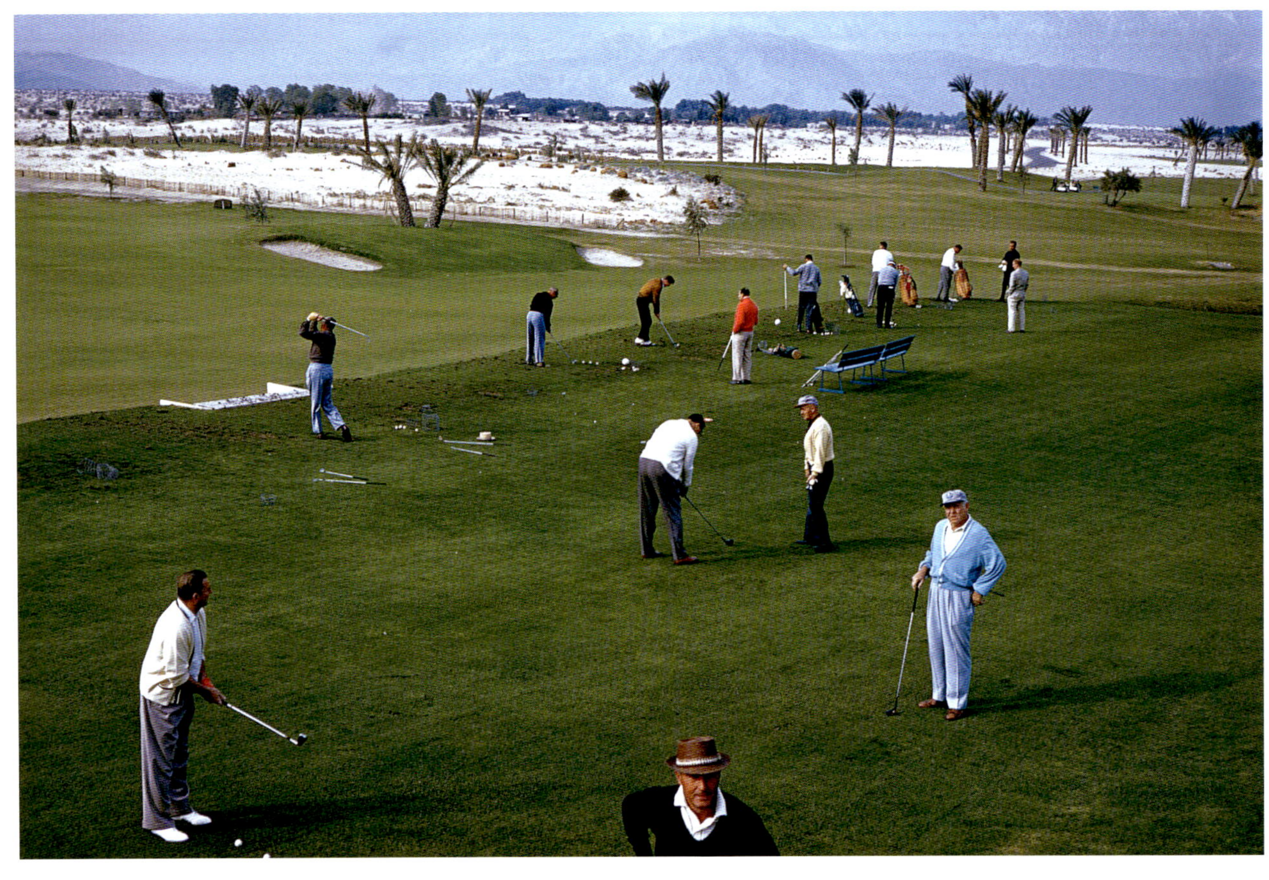

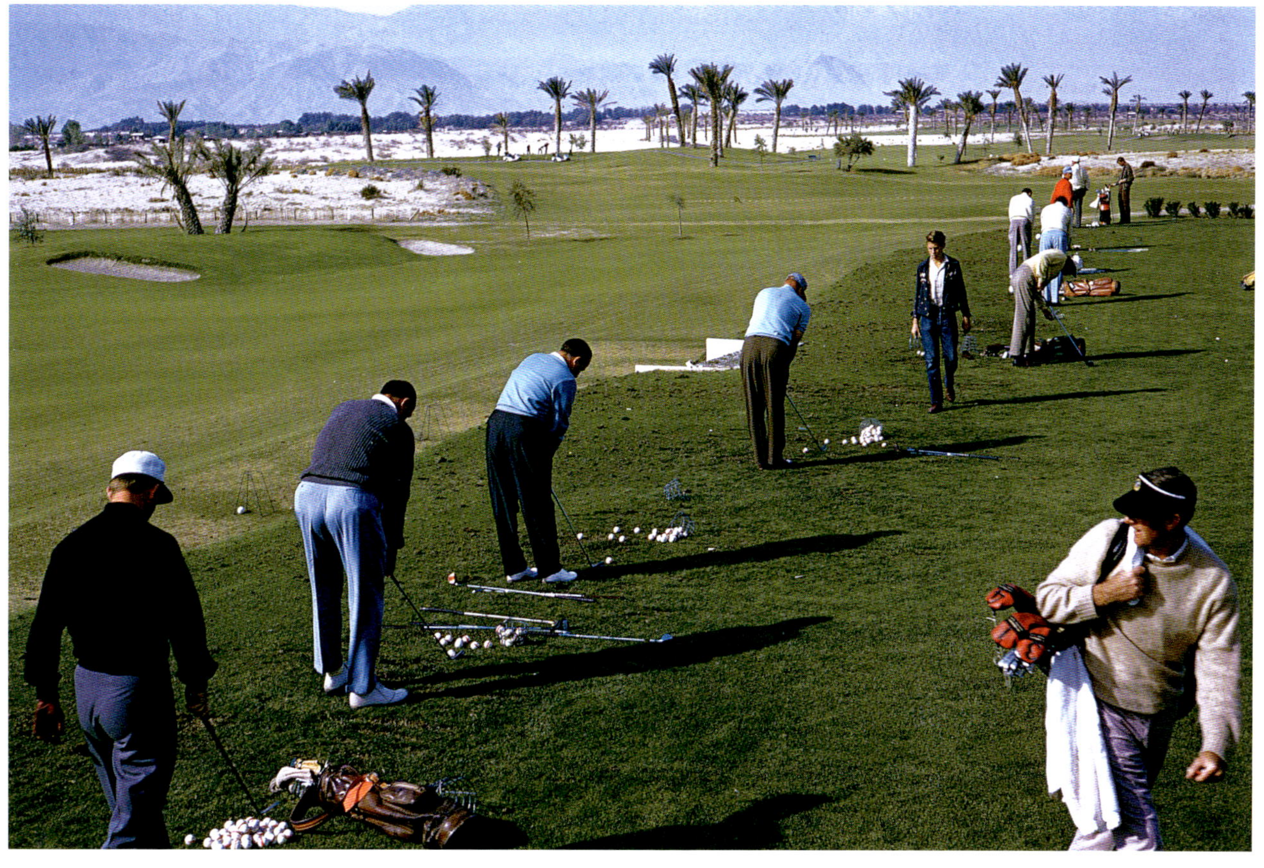

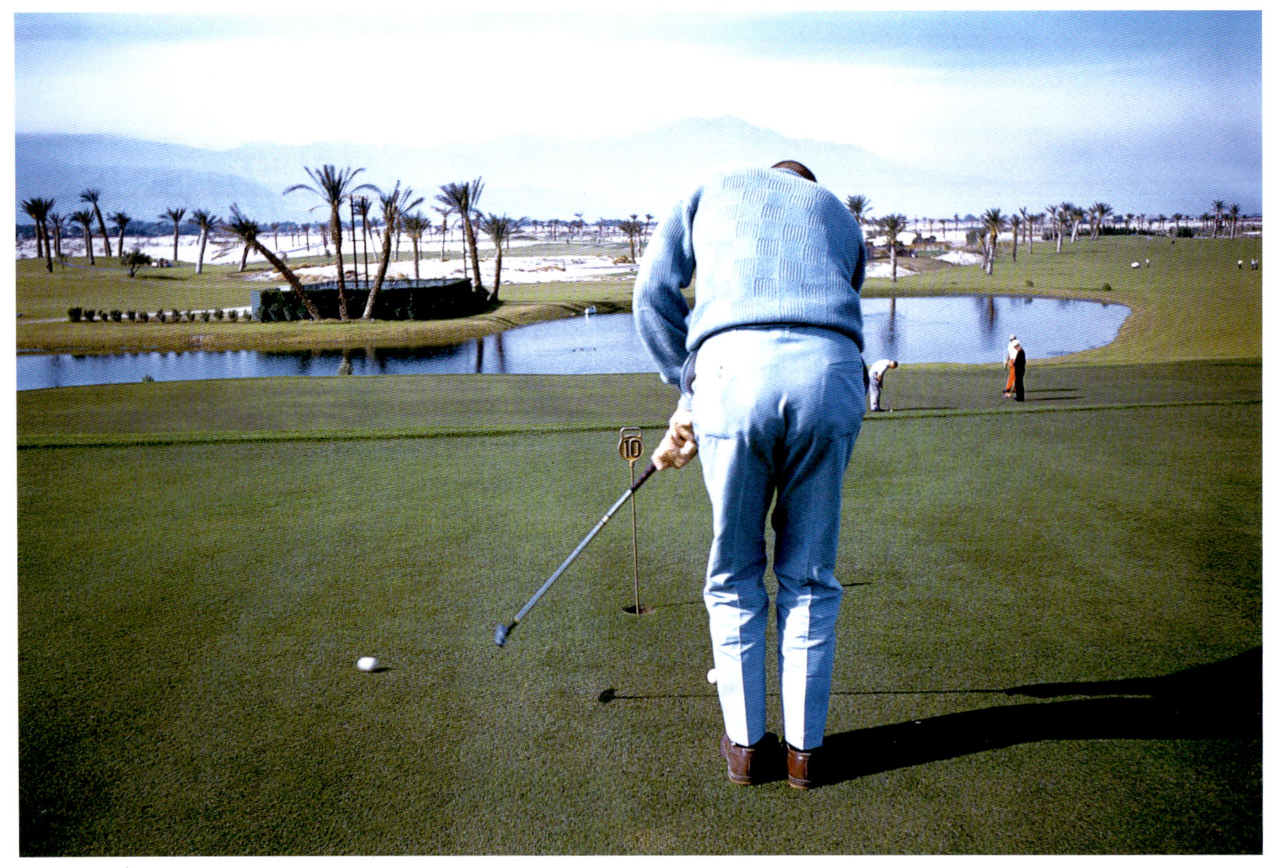
10

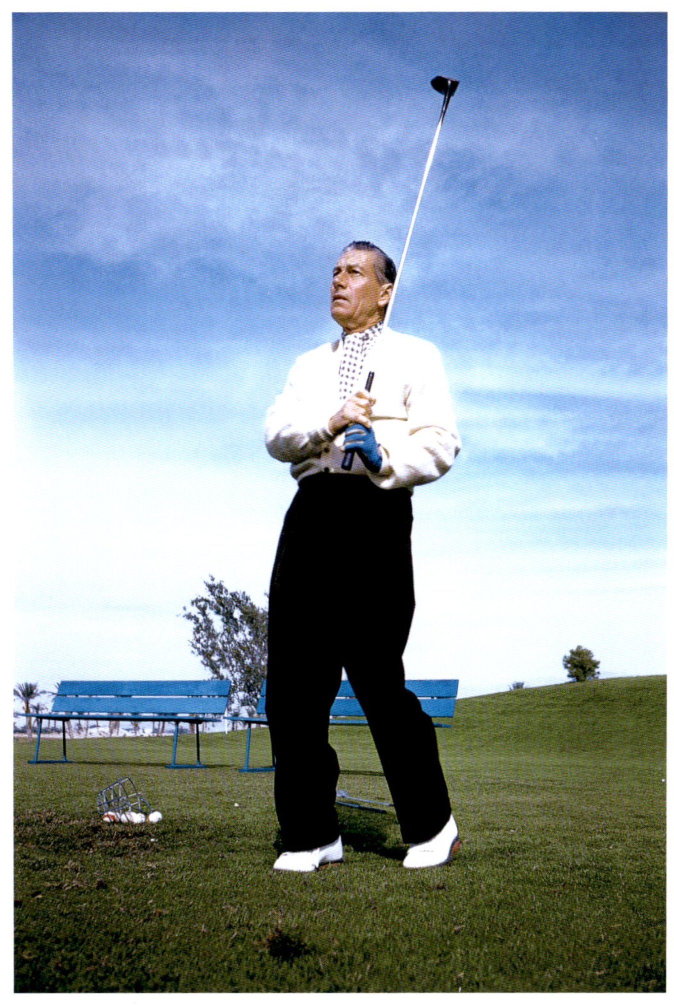

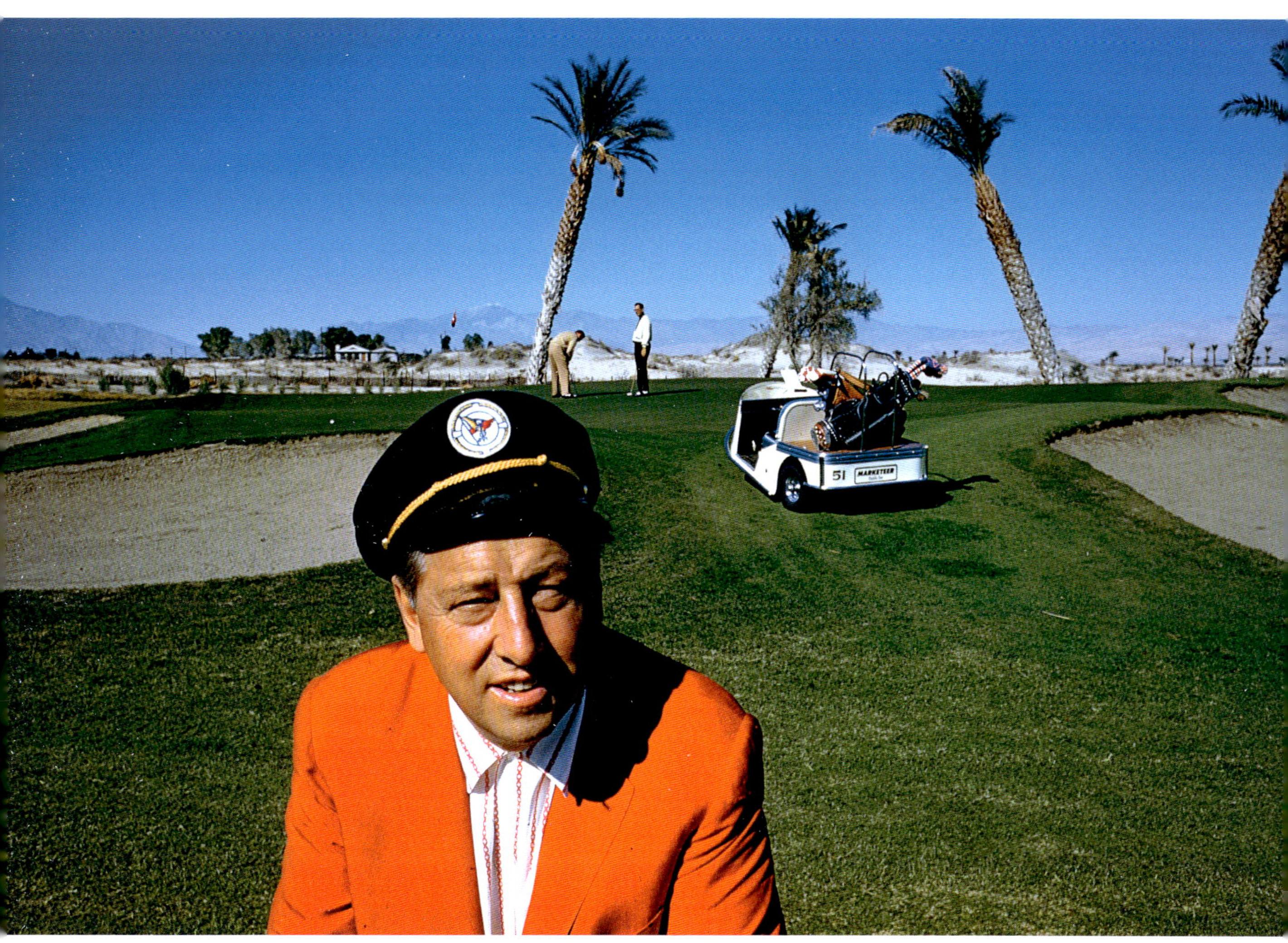
51
MARKETEER

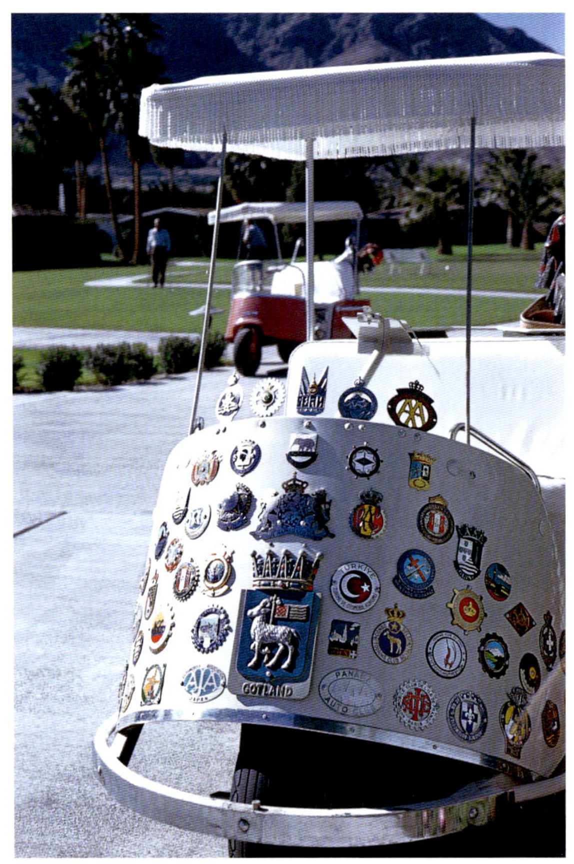
GOTLAND
TÜRKIYE

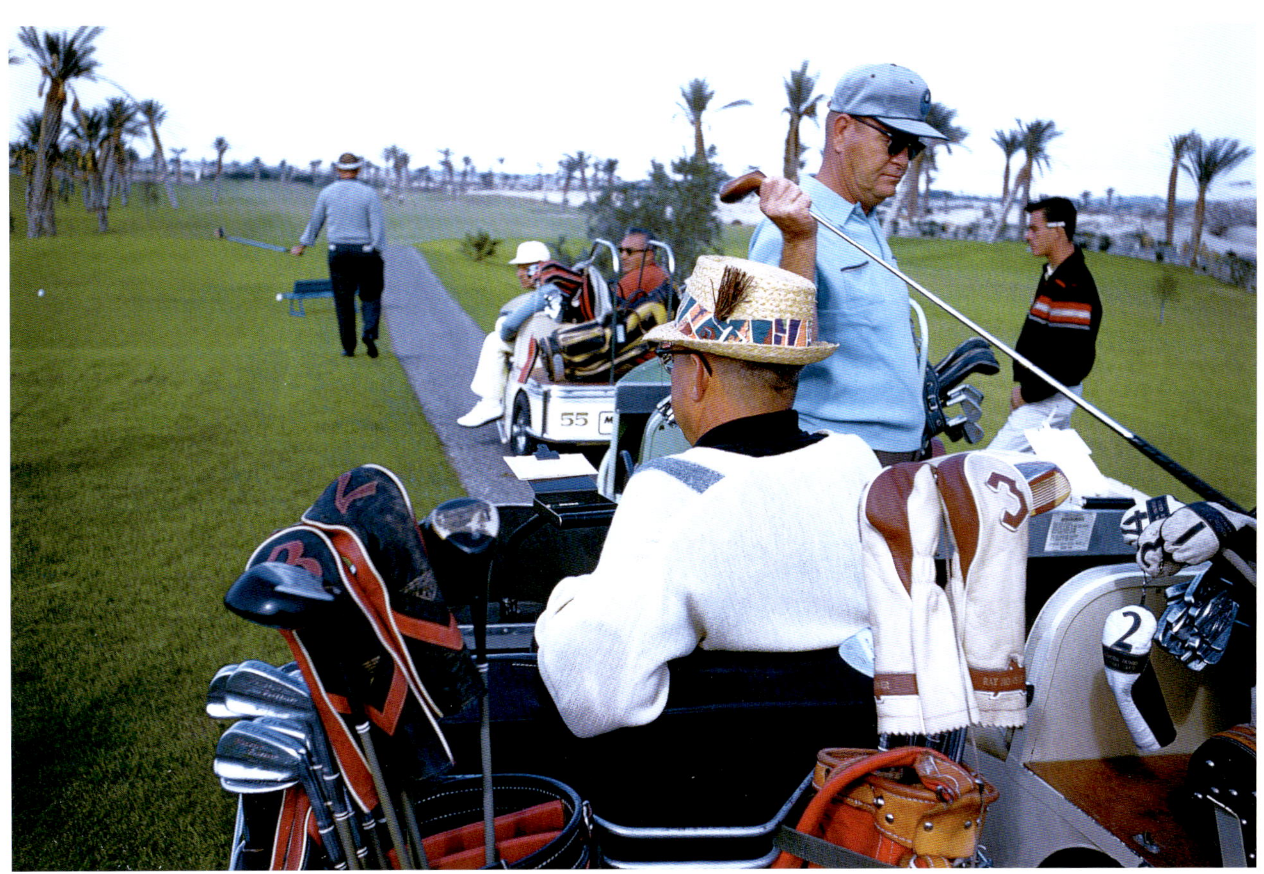

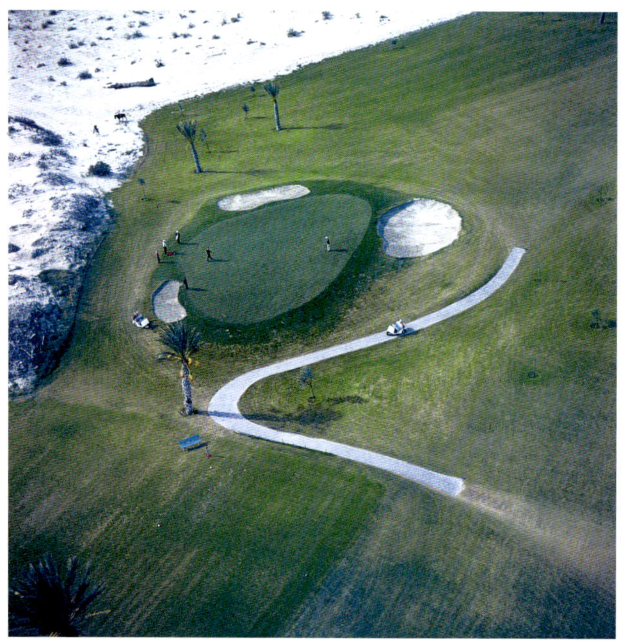

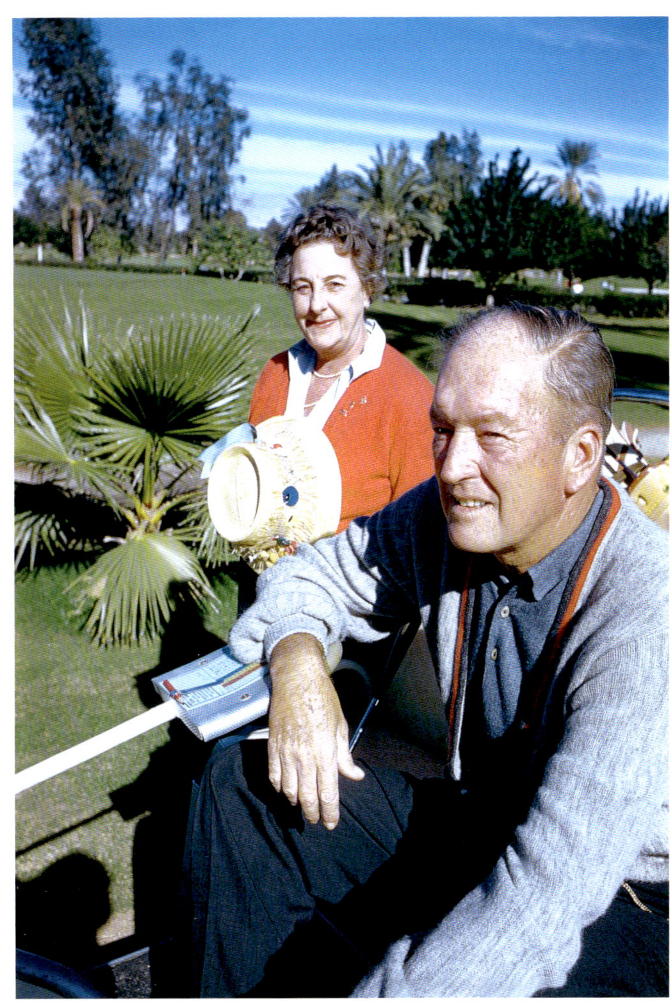

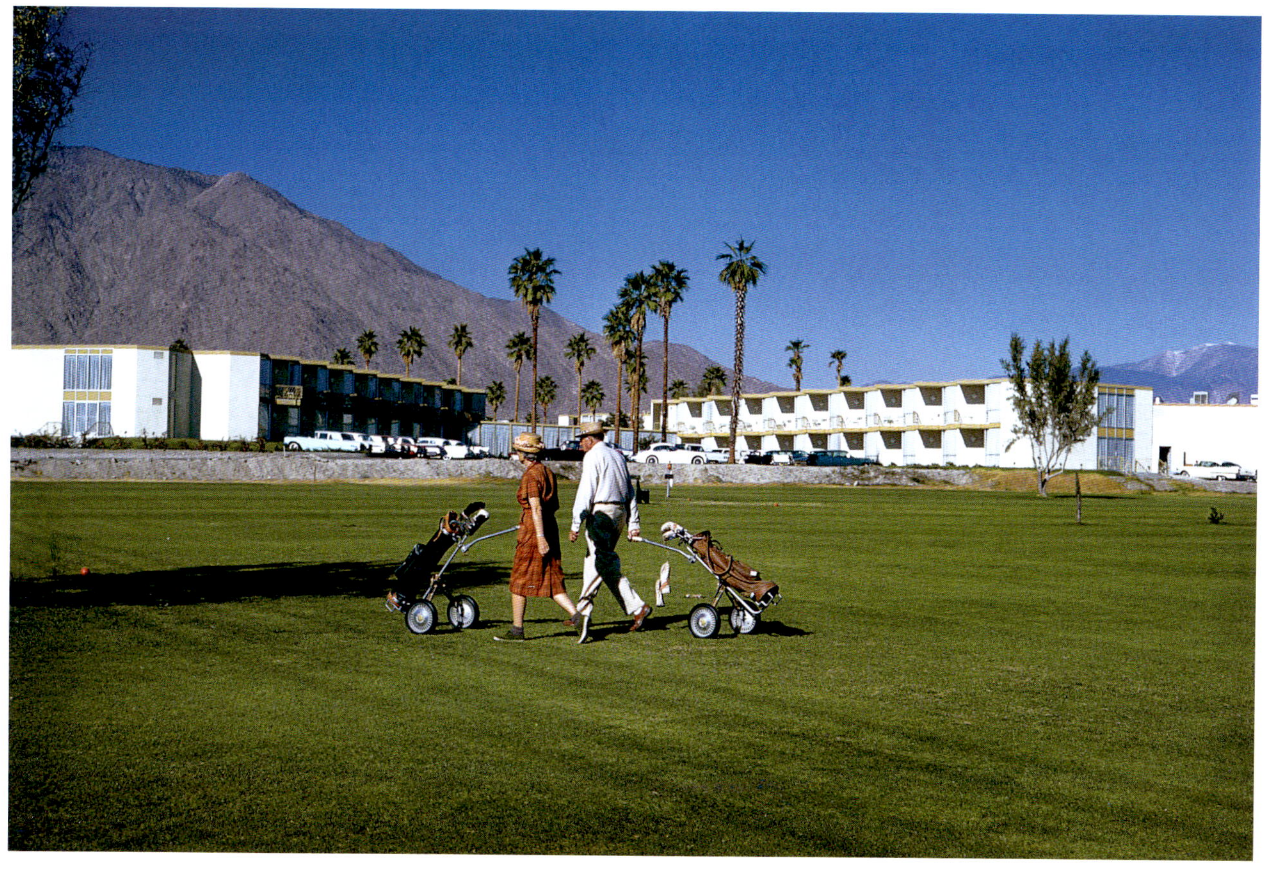

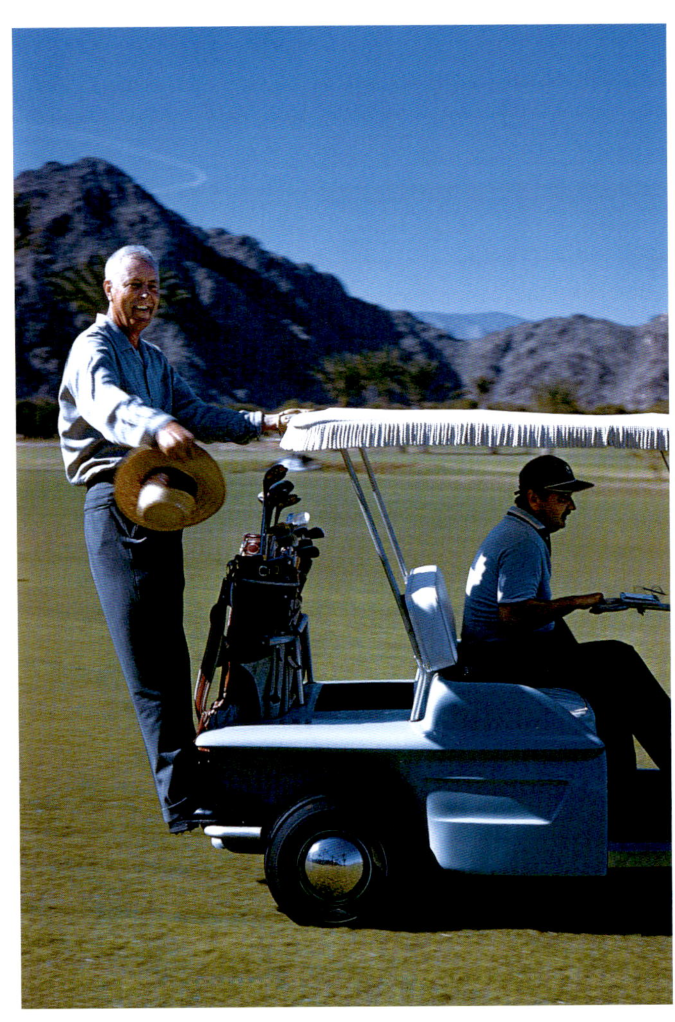

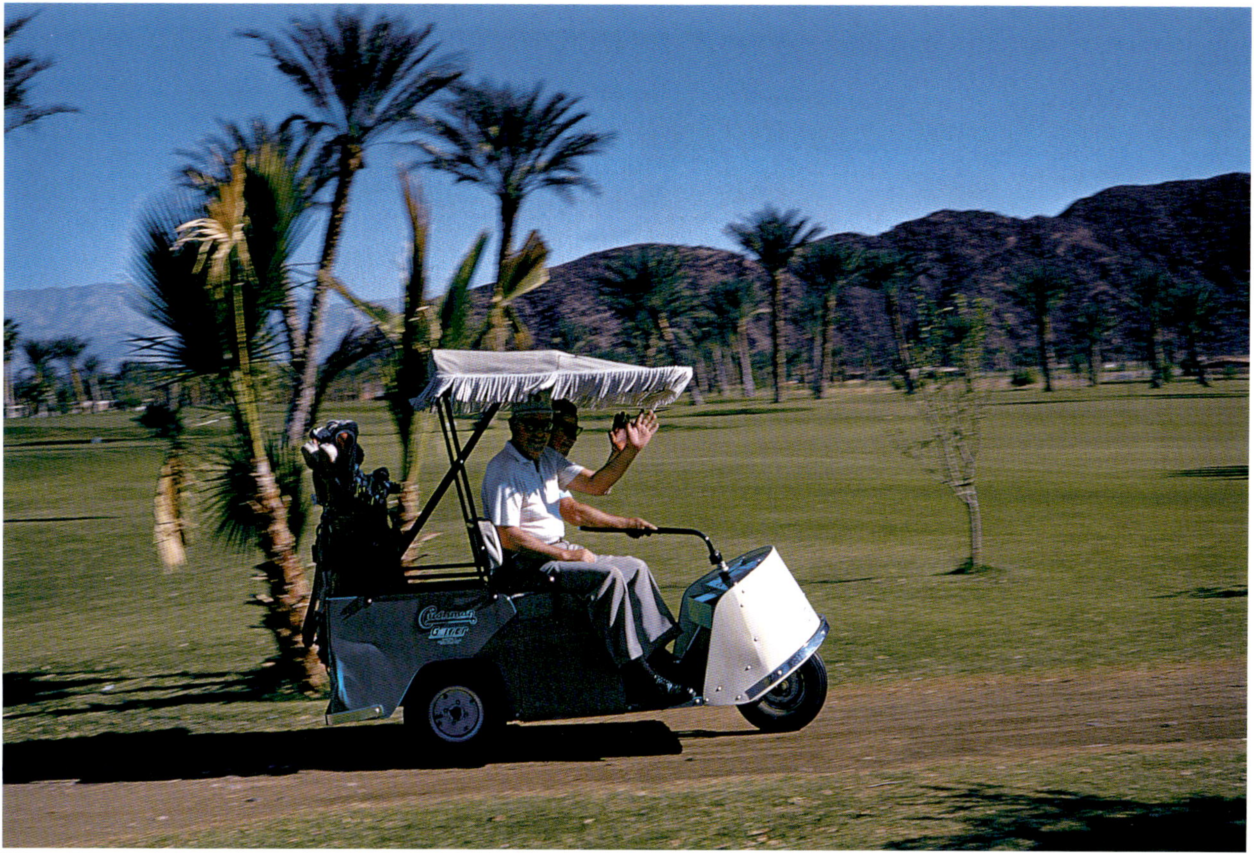

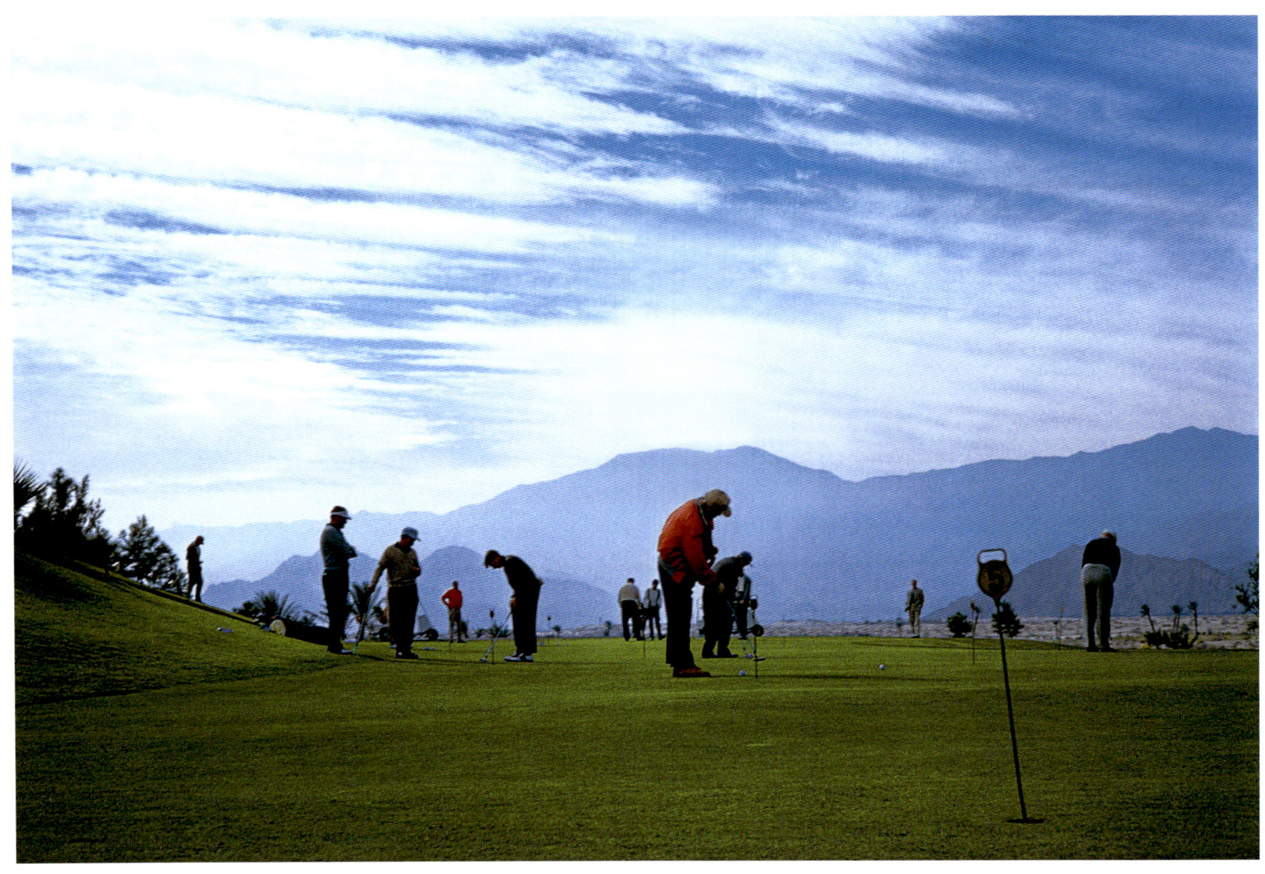

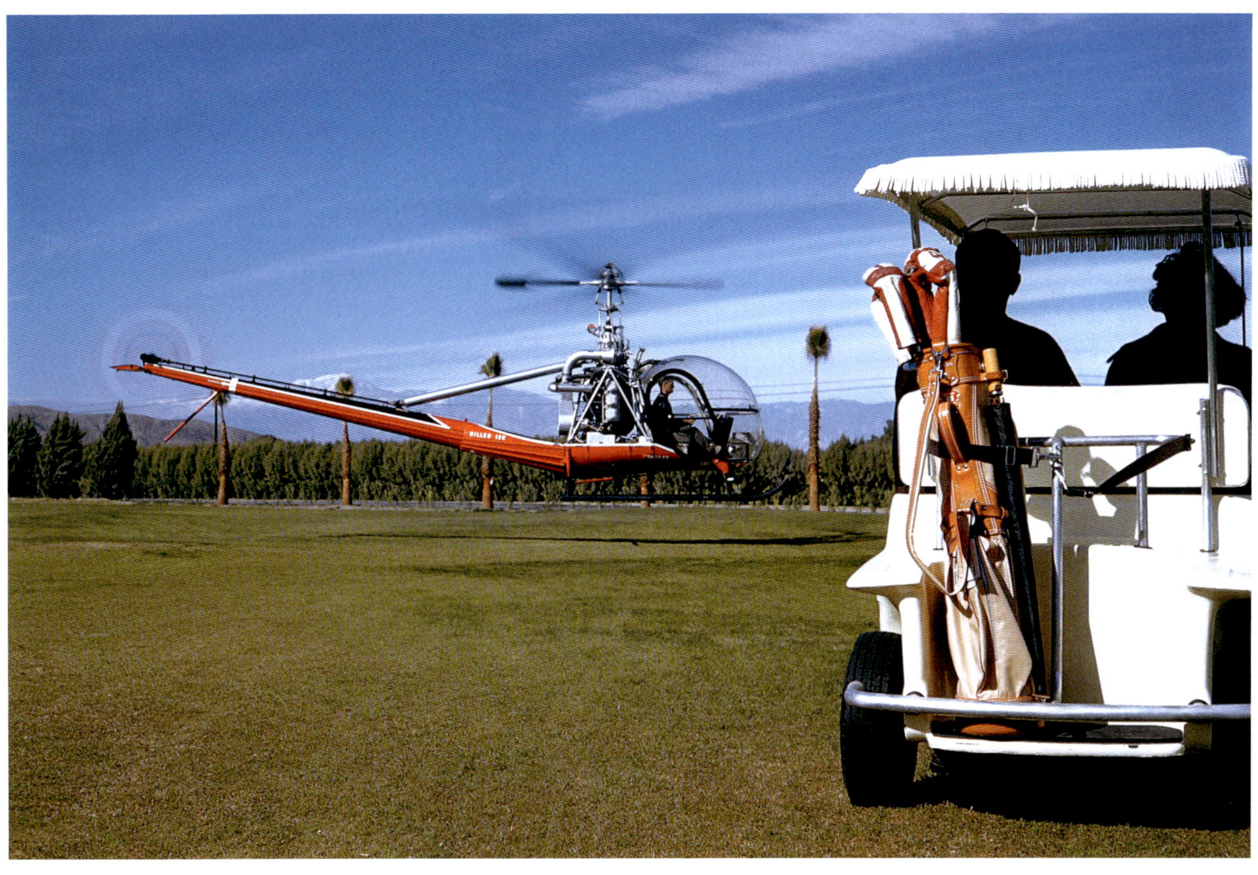

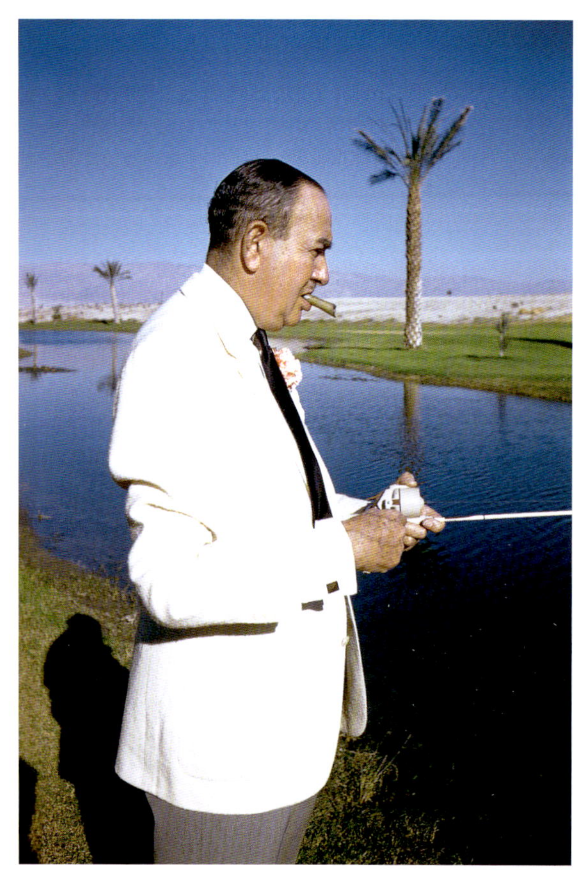

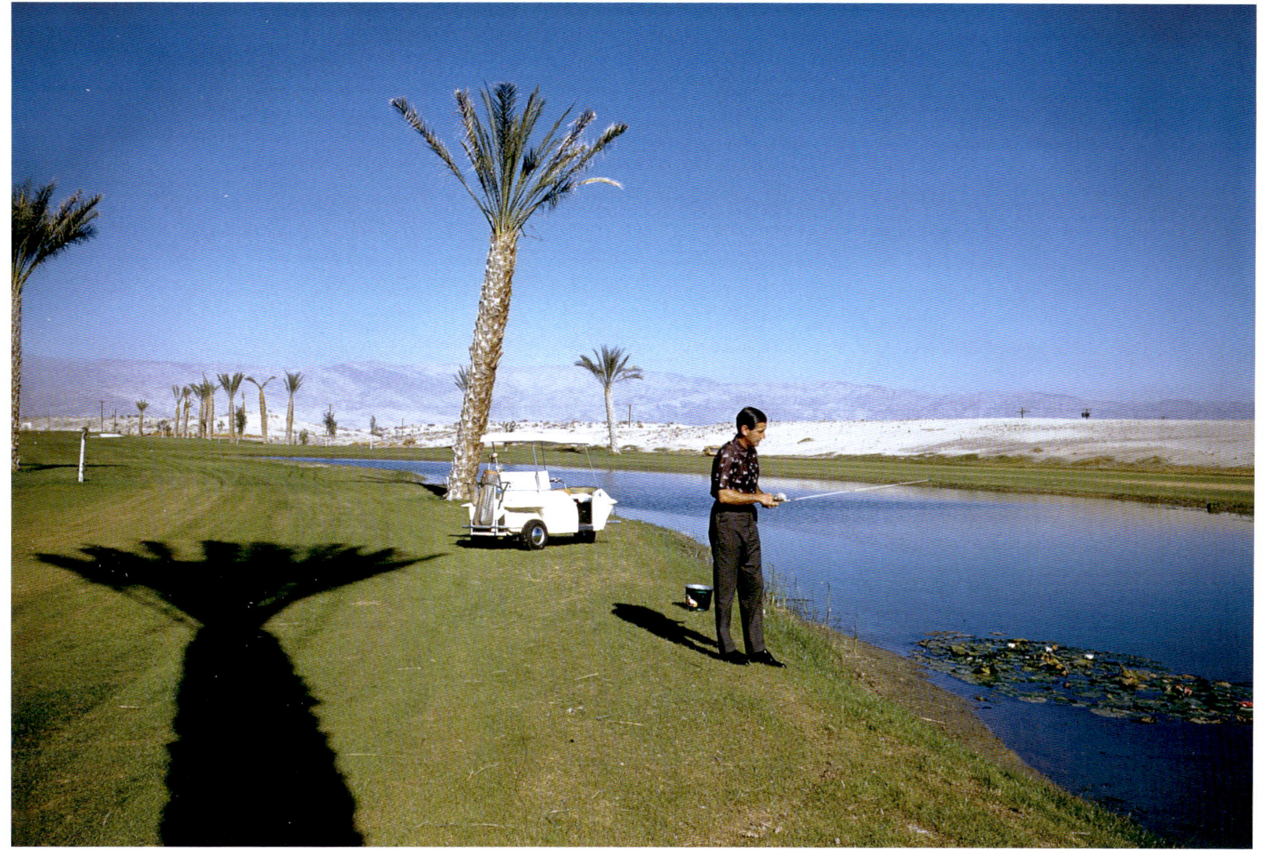

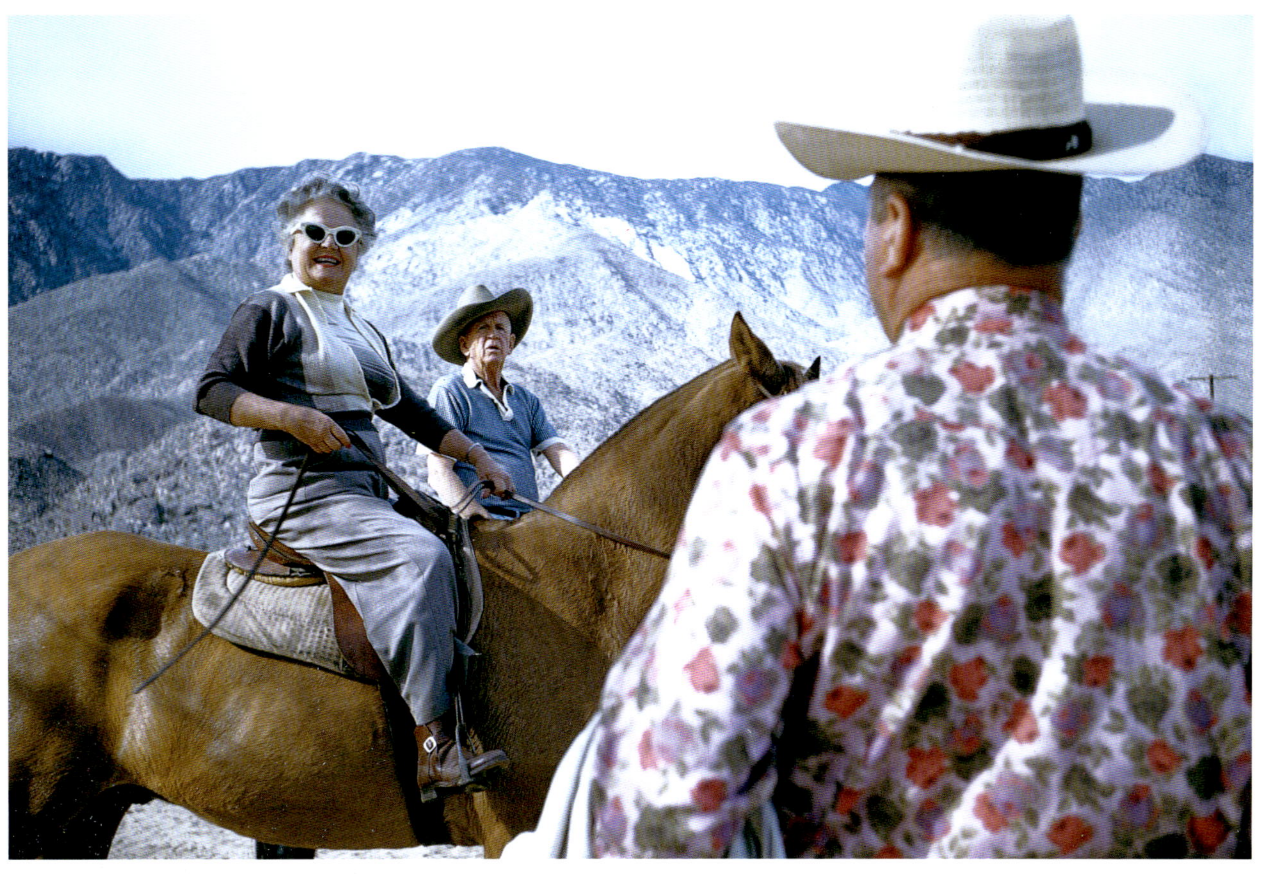

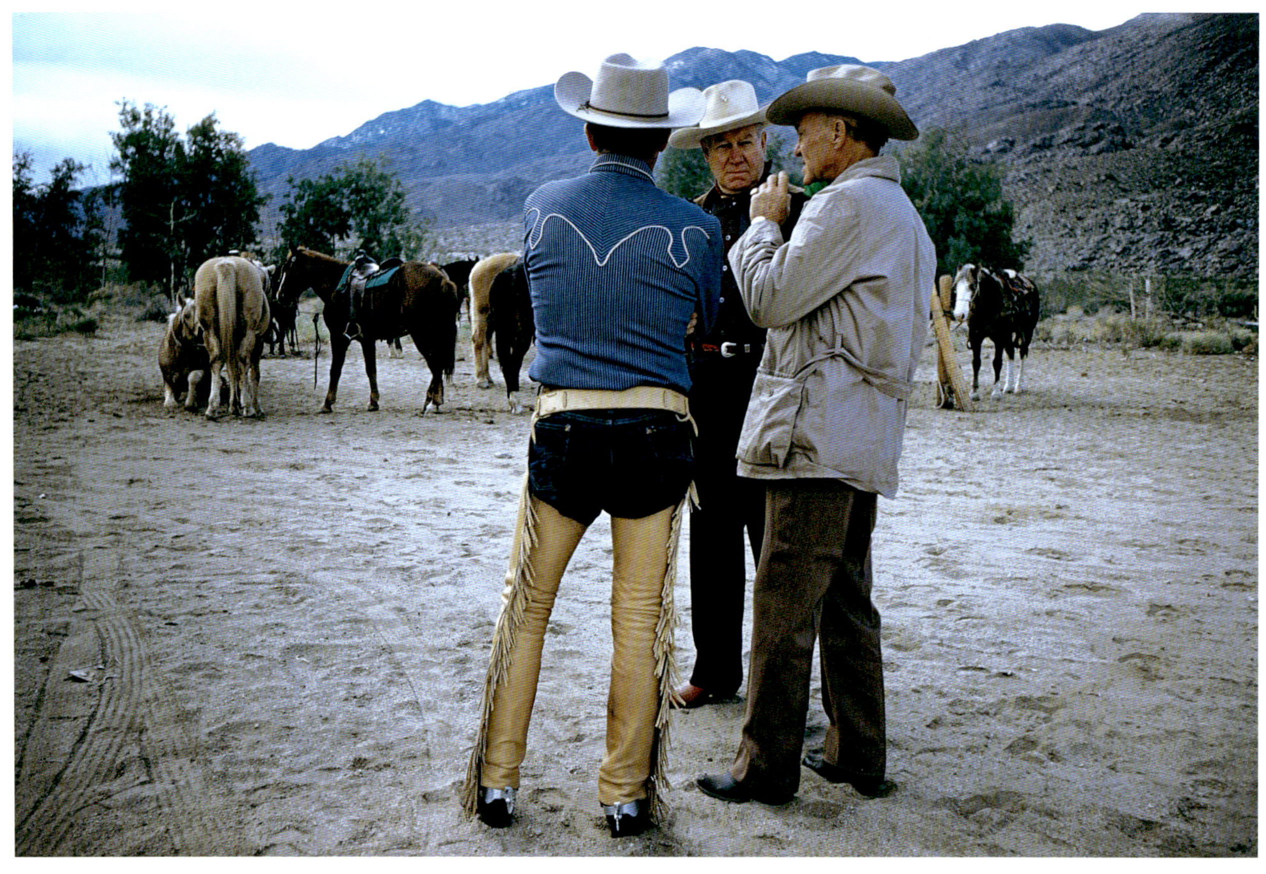

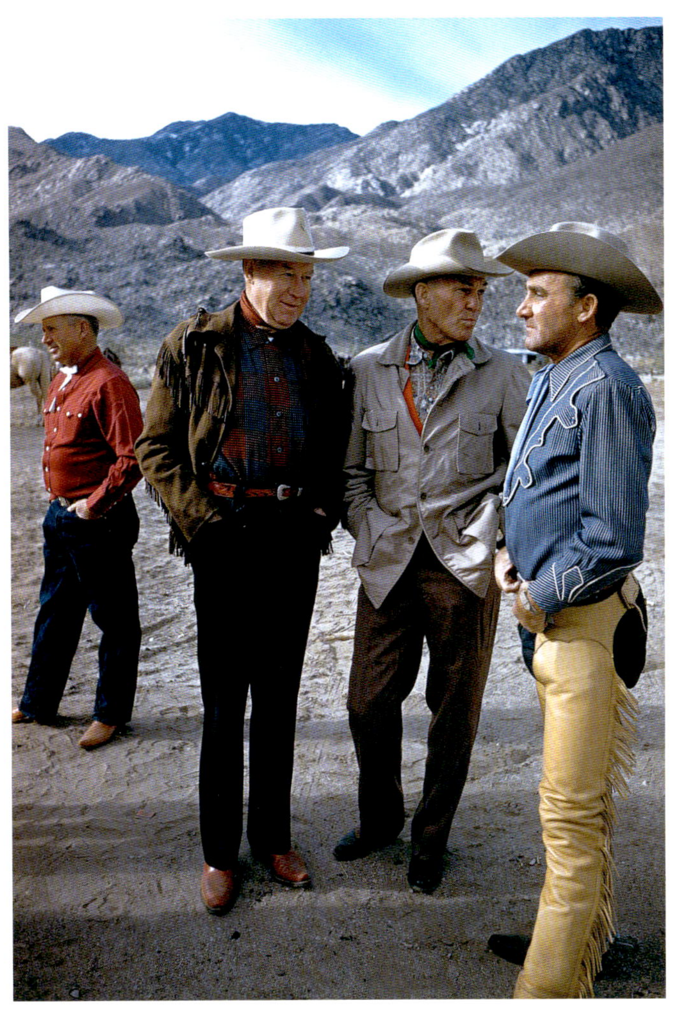

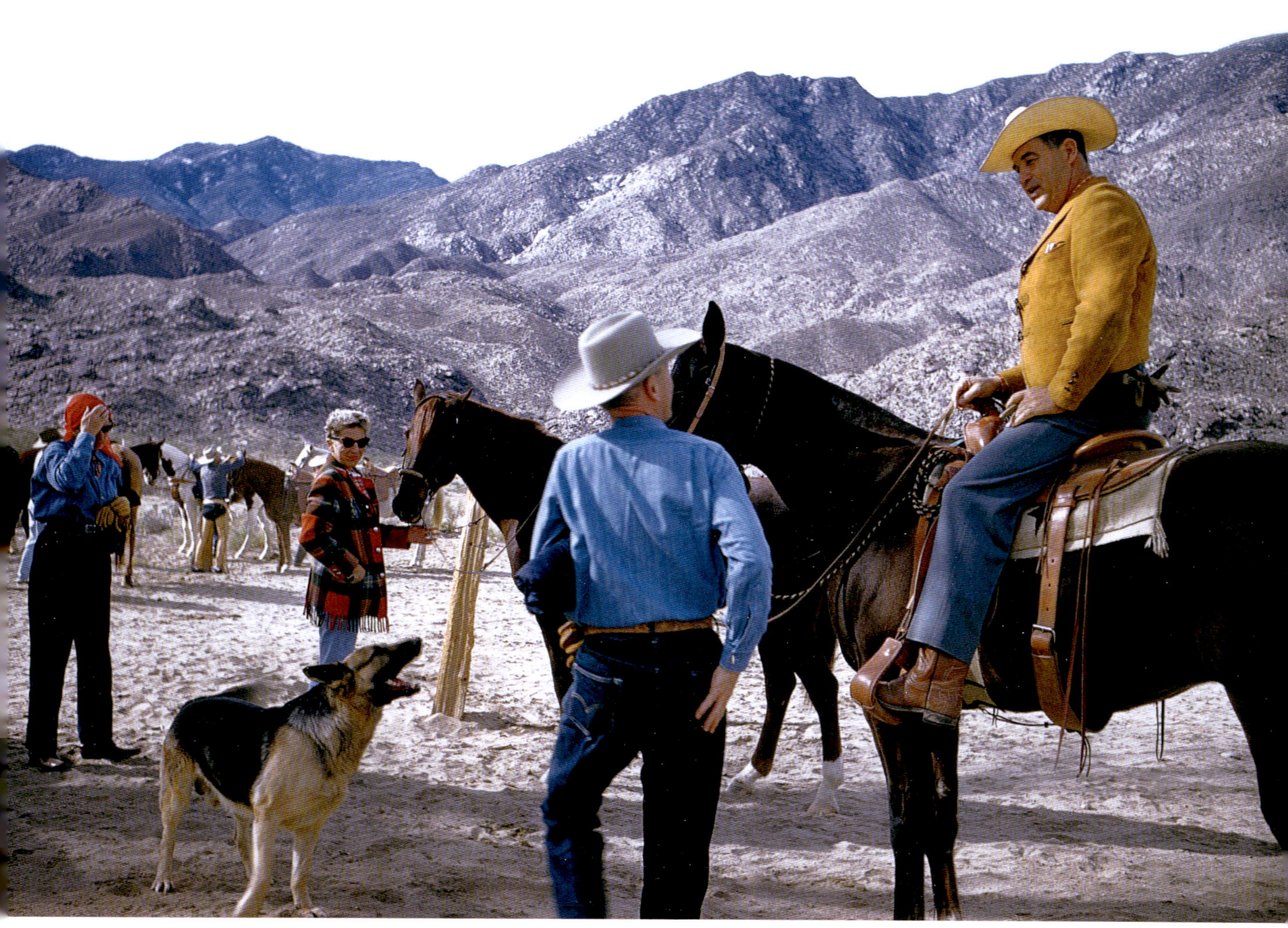

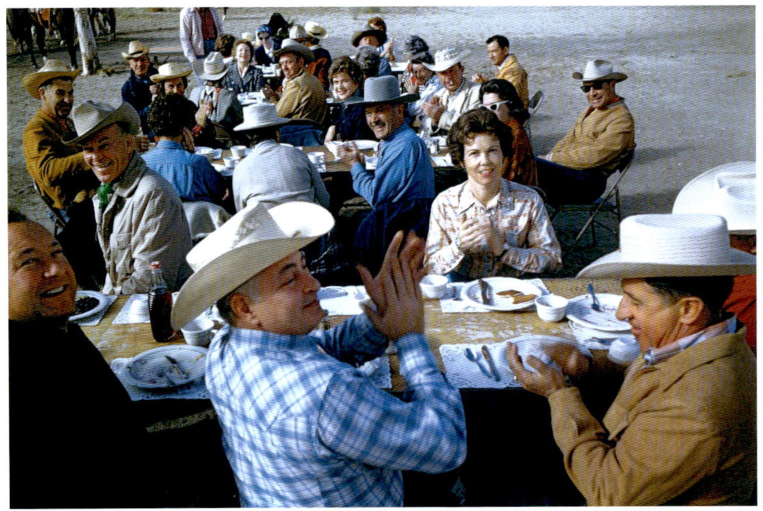

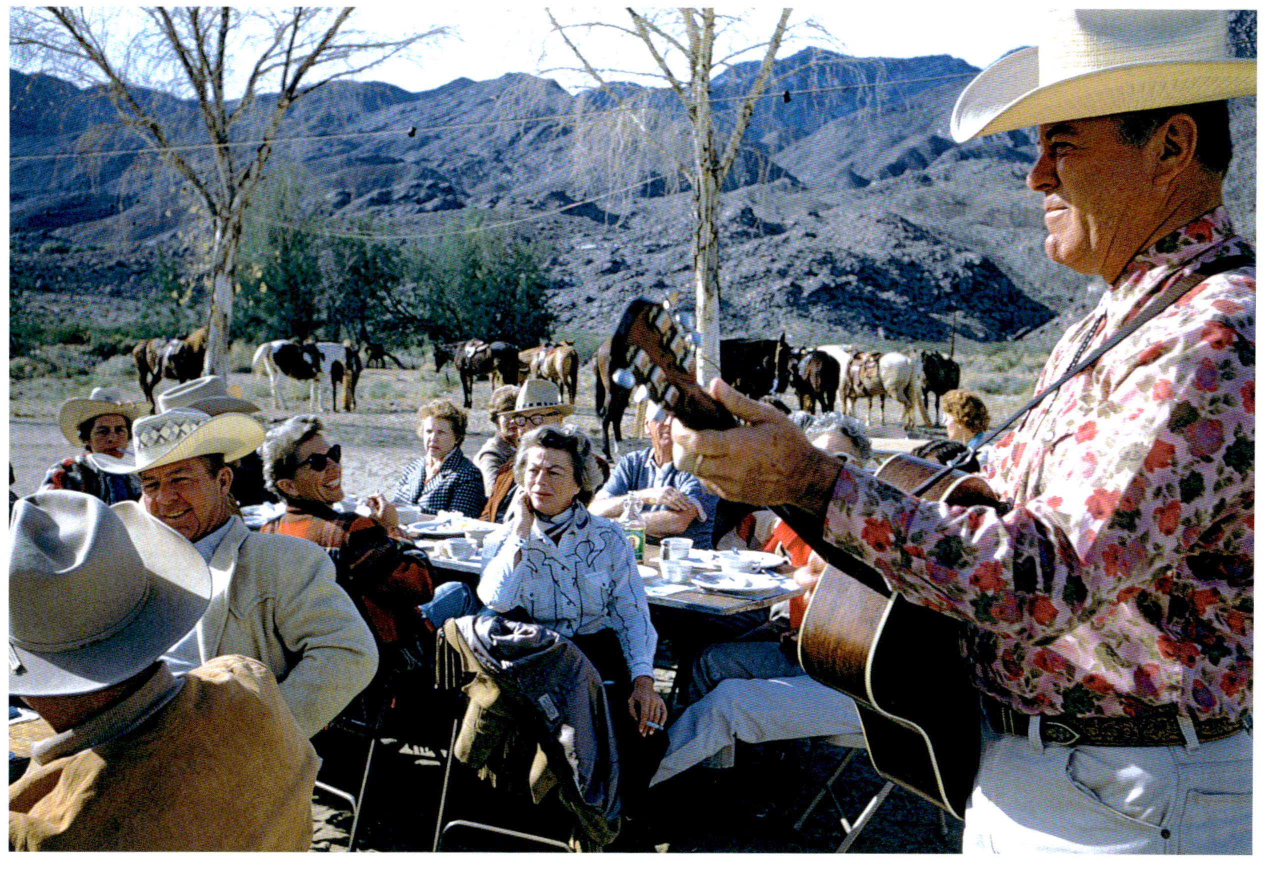

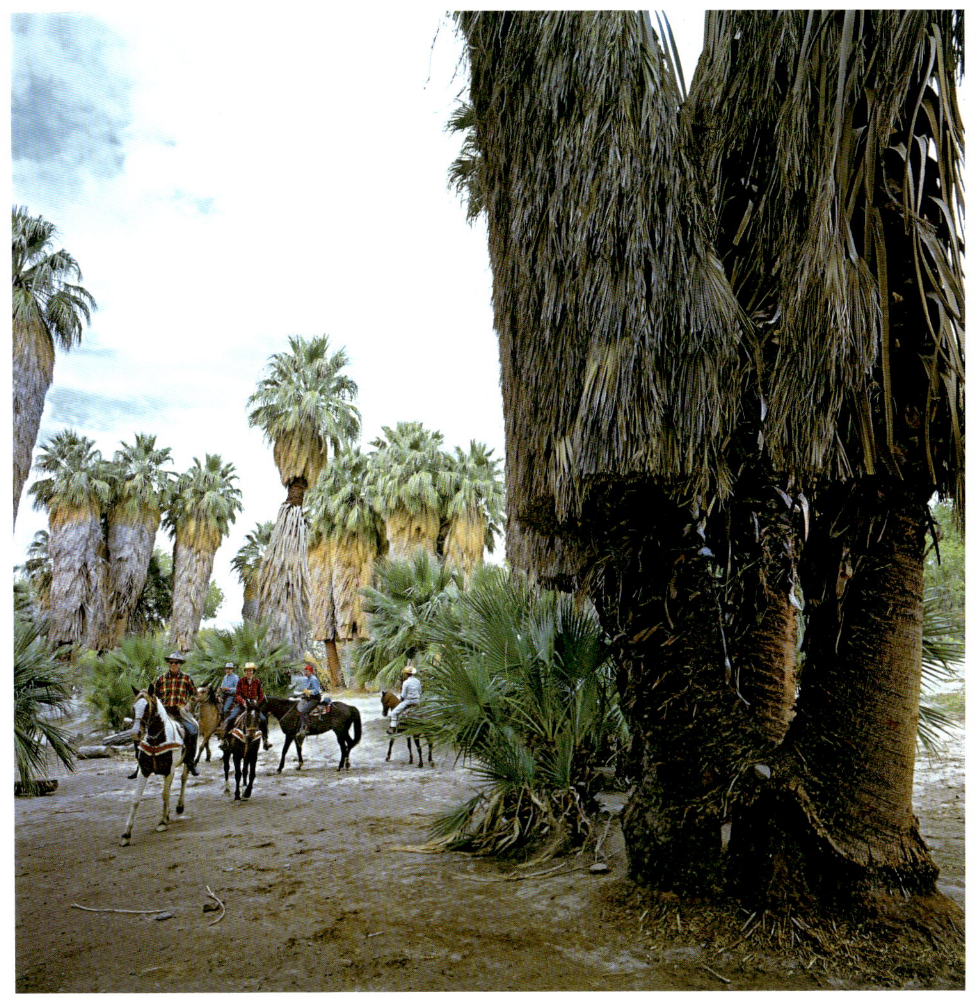

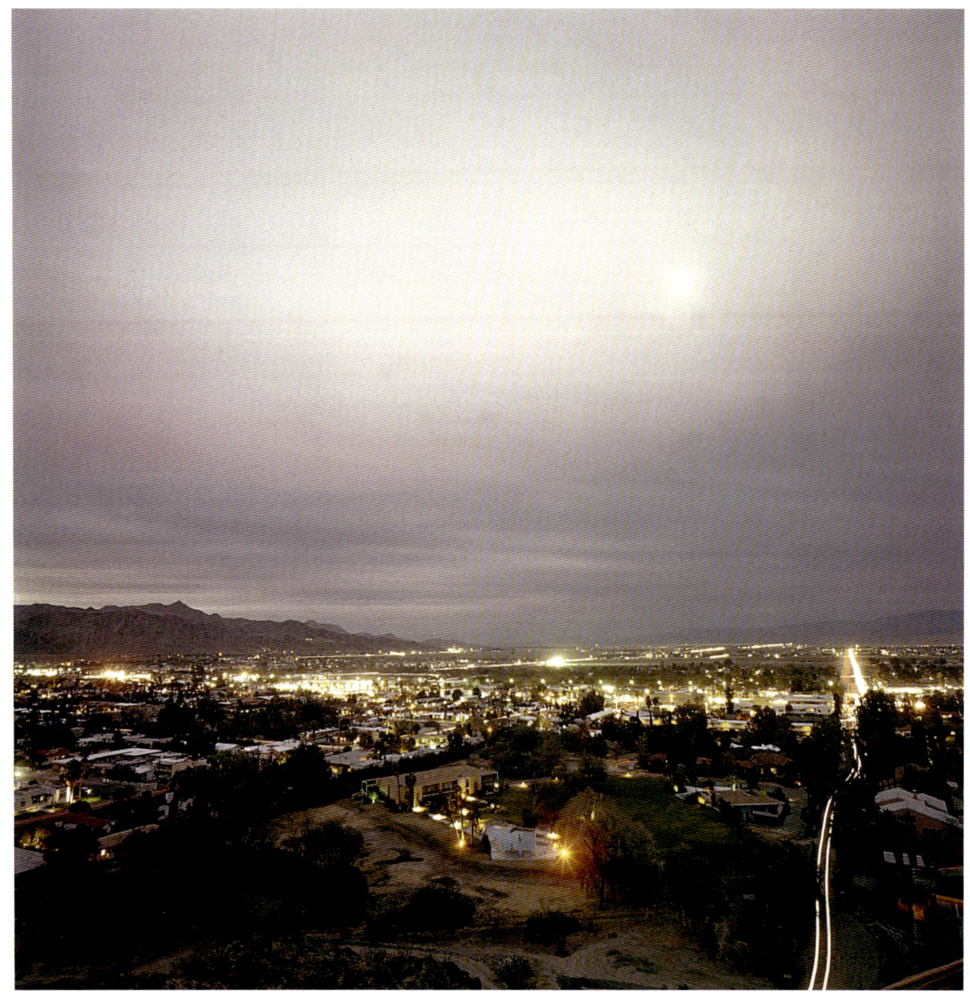

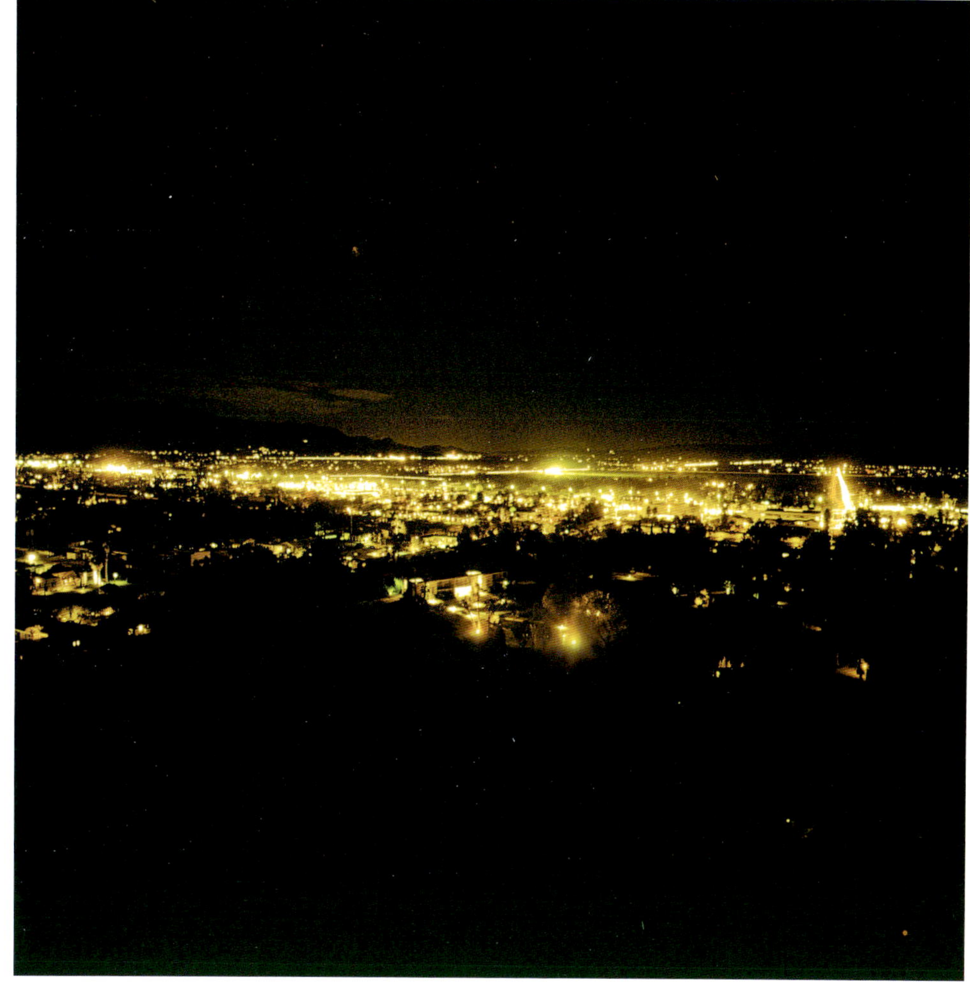

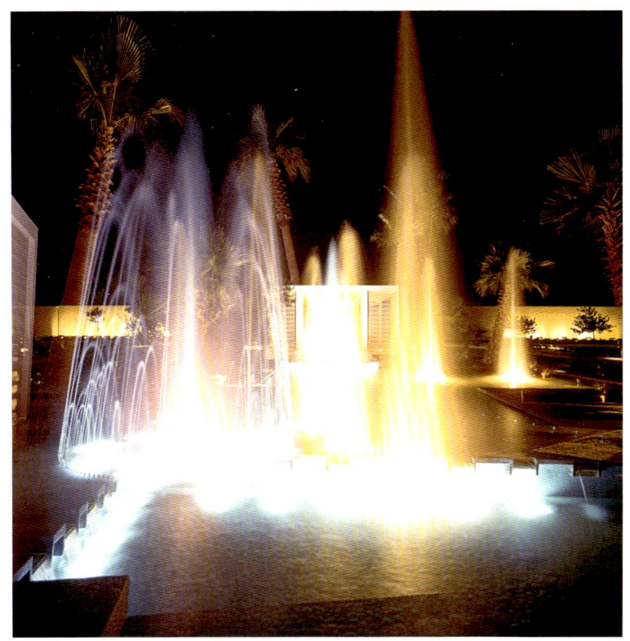

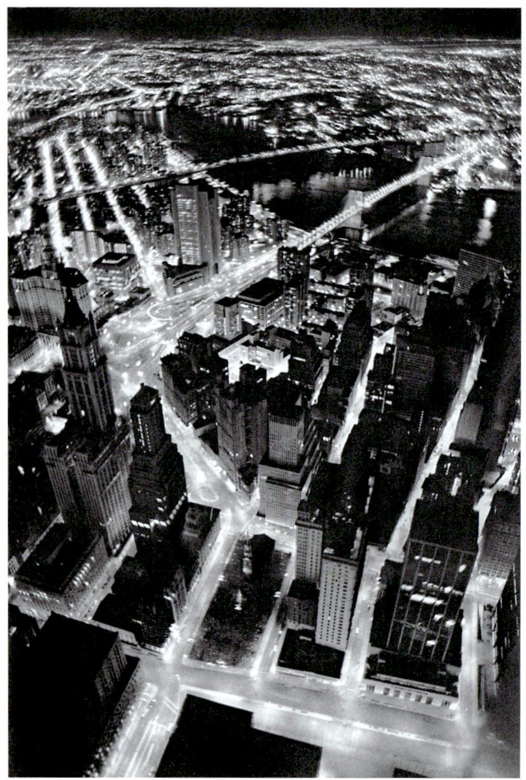

New York at night, April 1981.

AMERICA • Robert Doisneau

Robert Doisneau worked regularly with the American press after the war. His most famous photograph *Le Baiser de l'Hôtel de Ville* ("Kiss by the Hôtel de Ville"), was taken for a commission from *Life* magazine in 1950. Rapho often gave him commissions for *The New York Times*, *Life*, and *Fortune*.

His pictures were also shown in museums in the United States.

In 1948, he took part in an exhibition on French photography in New York with Édouard Boubat, André Papillon, and Willy Ronis.

In 1951, he showed at the MoMA in New York with Brassaï, Willy Ronis, Henri Cartier-Bresson, and Izis.

In 1960 however he still had not crossed the Atlantic. Due to a lack of finances, he let the photographs travel in his place.

From 1957, Robert Doisneau and Maurice Baquet worked together on a book whose first title was *On dirait du veau* ("Looks Like Veal") and then, the more reasonable *Violoncelle slalom* ("Cello Slalom"). They had already selected a large number of pictures and written a joyfully crazy, offbeat version of Maurice Baquet's biography.

In June 1960, Maurice Baquet left for New York to appear in *La Plume de ma tante* ("The Pen of My Aunt") by Robert Dhéry. The show was a great success and ran for several months on Broadway. As soon as he arrived, Maurice asked his friend Robert to come and join him in discovering New York, which enchanted him: the city's scenery proved to be a source of inspiration for the photographer, which allowed them to take their book project further.

Robert Doisneau talked about it to Raymond Grosset, the director of the Rapho agency, who immediately notified Charles Rado, the founder of the Parisian agency located since the war in New York, where he had founded the Rapho-Guillemette agency.

Thanks to the efficiency of the two collaborating agents, commissions were not long in coming.

Robert Doisneau took his first flight to the United States on November 19, 1960, to take pictures for *Fortune* magazine. The theme of his photoreport was the building of golf courses in Palm Springs, a refuge for rich retired Americans in the Colorado desert.

After a day in New York, he arrived in Palm Springs on November 21.

He stayed until December 1. What he discovered there incited him to go far beyond the report's theme. Taking the subject beyond the encroachment of golfing greens on this arid land, he drew an amusing portrait of an artificial planet repainted in the softest of colors. He used a Rolleiflex, a Leica, and a Hasselblad in turn and used color film for purely aesthetic reasons for the first time.

On December 2 he was in the Paramount Studios in Hollywood where Jerry Lewis was making *The Ladies Man*. A week of photographing followed, which was complicated by the American trade union's rule that all foreign photographers should be shadowed by an American colleague.

Robert Doisneau left Los Angeles on December 9 to finally join Maurice Baquet in New York, where they made, as they had dreamed, a series of photographs, continuing until December 17 when Doisneau returned to Paris. A snow-covered New York provided them with superb scenes . . . which, however, were not enough to convince the publishers.

First begun in 1957, the book was published twenty-five years later by Georges Herscher under the title *Ballade pour violoncelle et chambre noire* ("Ballad for Cello and Black Box"). Decrescendo, time out.

Robert Doisneau returned to the United States twice.

In March 1966, for a photoreport commission in Montreal, Doisneau saw Charles Rado again in New York, where he spent three days essentially getting to know Wall Street. And he returned in April 1981 for an exhibition at the Witkin Gallery. A friendly trip in the company of Barbara Grosset and Willy Ronis. On this occasion he met the great portrait photographer Arnold Newman in his Manhattan studio.

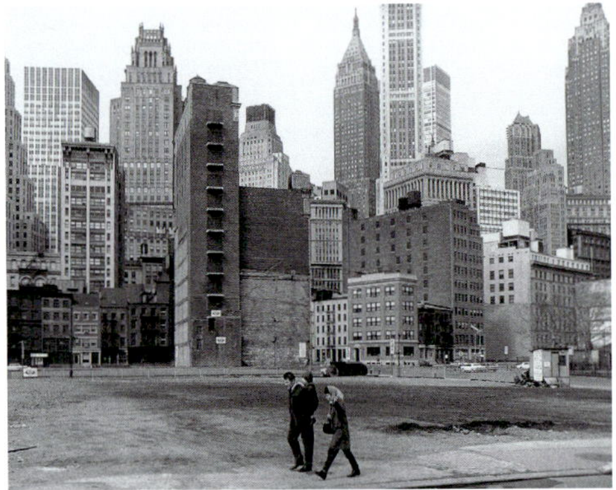

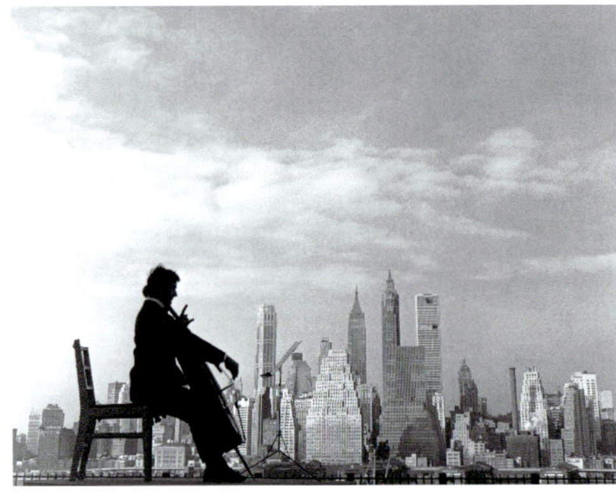

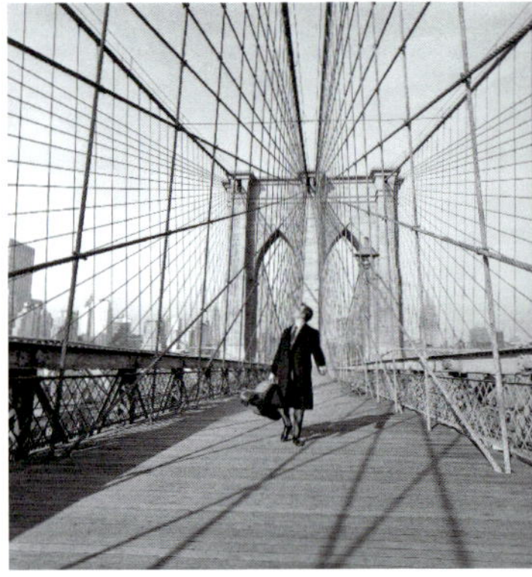

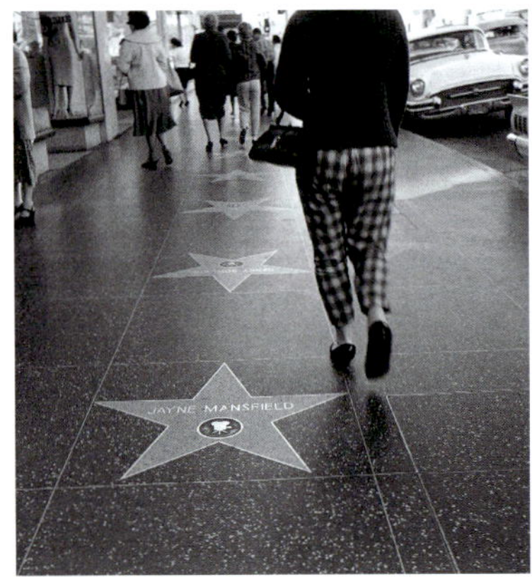

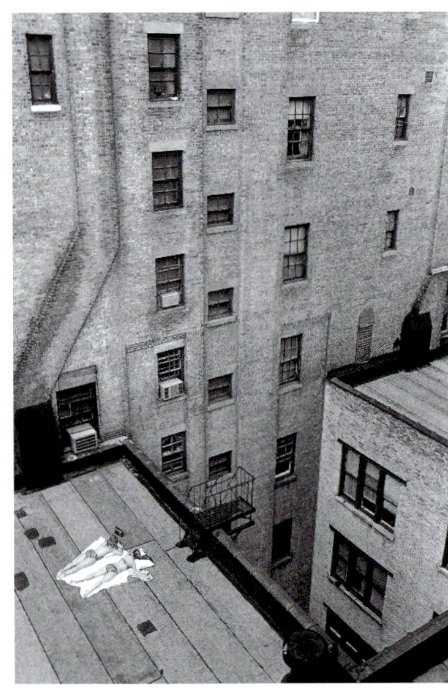

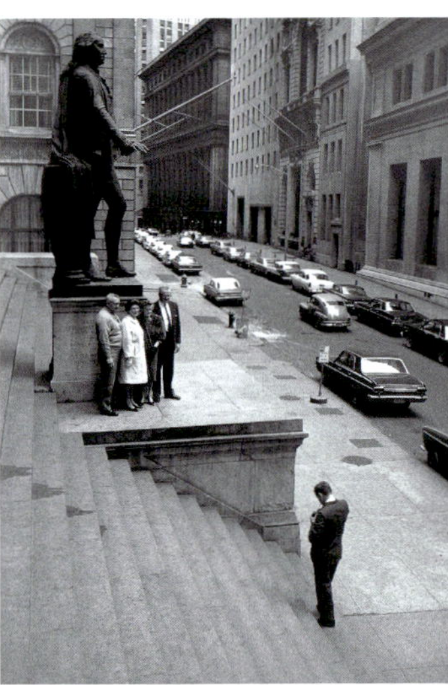

FROM TOP LEFT TO BOTTOM RIGHT
Walk with Charles Rado, New York, March 20, 1966. / Maurice Baquet, *Aubade pour Manhattan*, New York, December 1960. / Maurice Baquet on Brooklyn Bridge, New York, December 1960. / Jayne Mansfield's star, Los Angeles, November 1960. / From Arnold Newman's studio, New York, April 26, 1981. / Family photo on Wall Street, New York, March 1966.

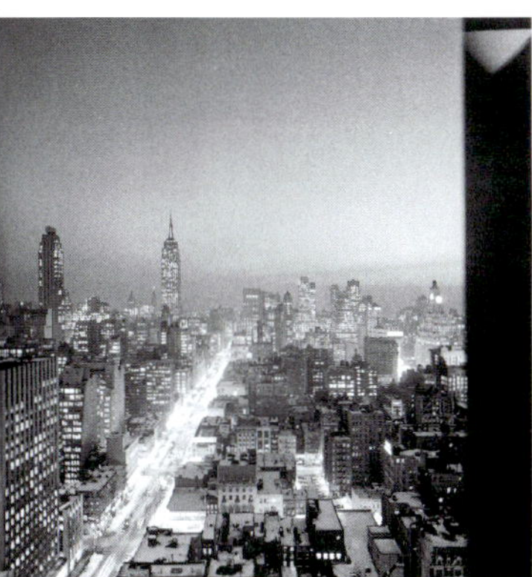

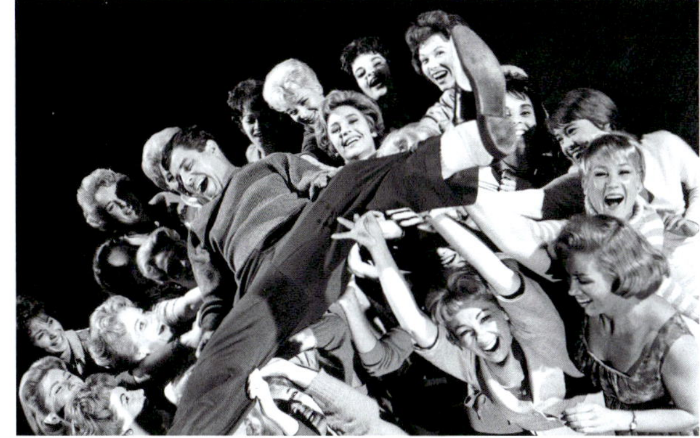

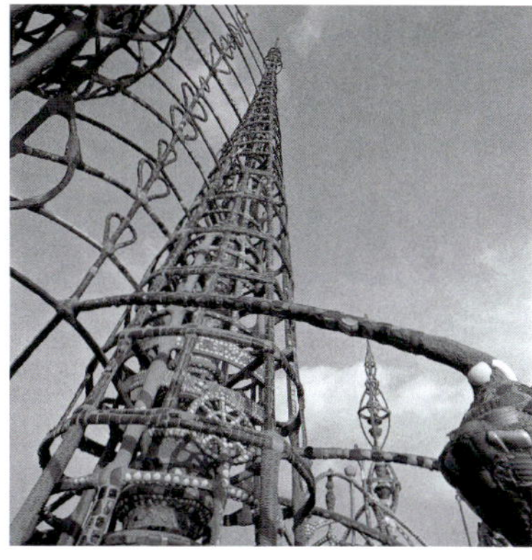

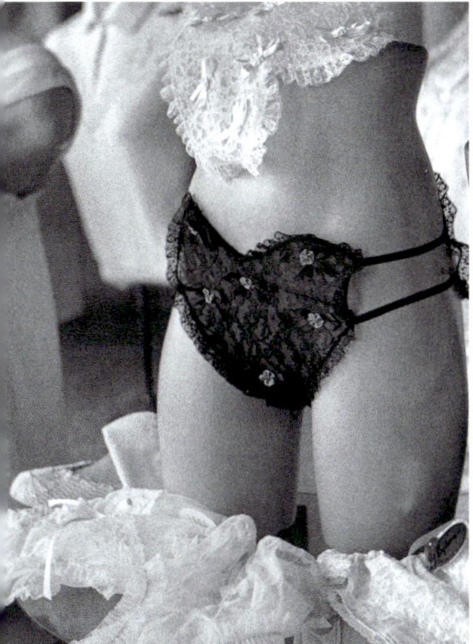

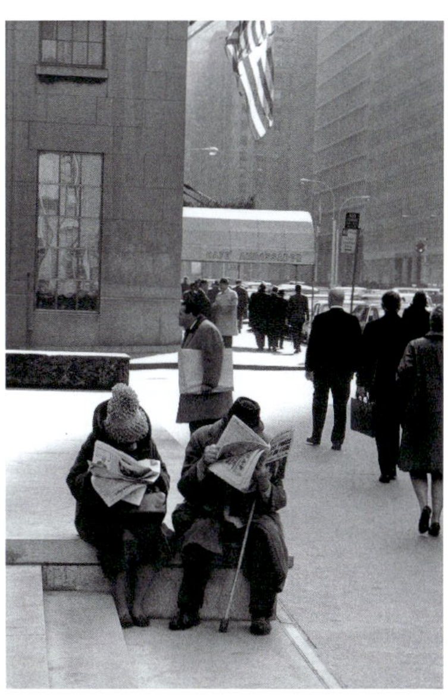

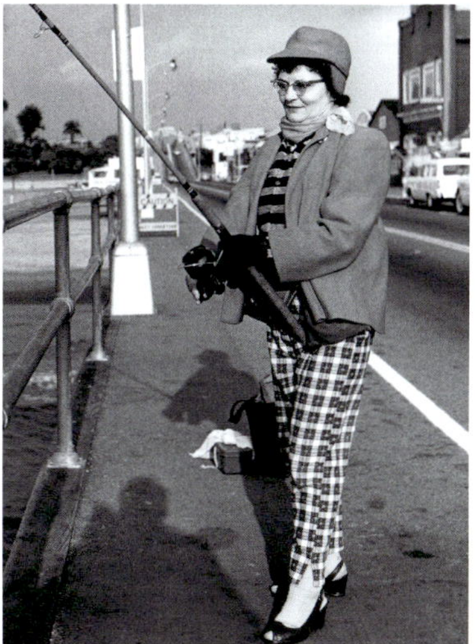

FROM TOP LEFT TO BOTTOM RIGHT
New York at night, December 1960. / Jerry Lewis in *The Ladies Man* in Hollywood, December 2, 1960. / Simon Rodia's buildings, Los Angeles, December 4, 1960. / Californian underwear, November 1960. / Reading the newspaper in Wall Street, New York, March 1966. / California, December 1960.

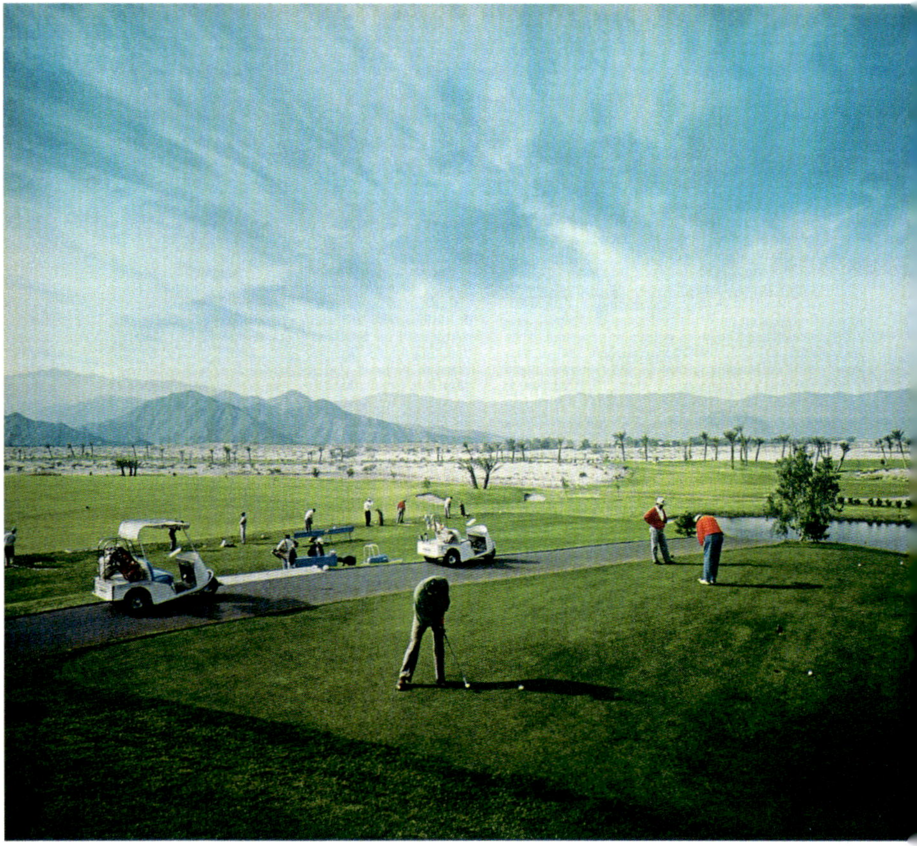

At Bermuda Dunes, one of the resort's twelve country clubs, golfers sharpen their putting and driving. Average midday temperature in winter: 82°.

PALM SPRINGS: GREEN AND PLAYFUL GROWS THE DESERT

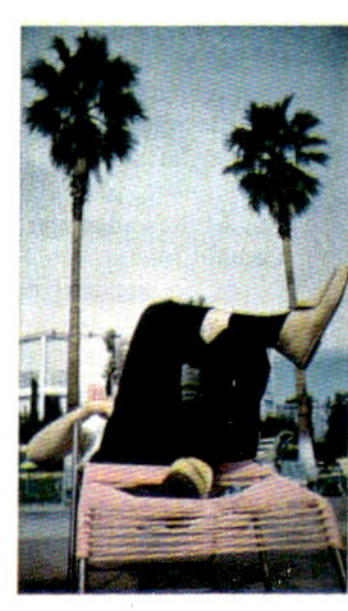

122 FORTUNE *February 1961*

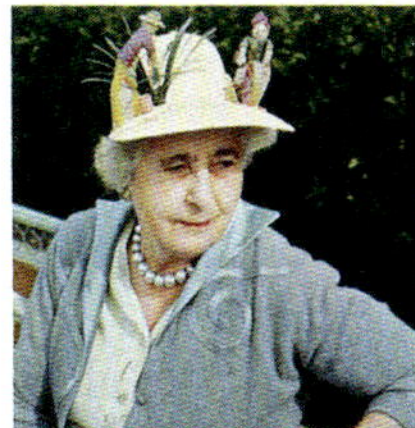

Mrs. C. W. Stimson, of Portland, Oregon, a visitor for eighteen years.

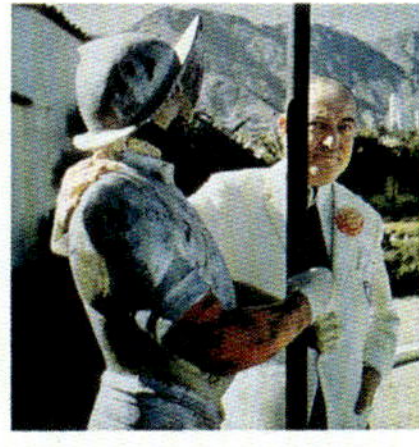

John Elsbach, of La Quinta Country Club, and wooden conquistador.

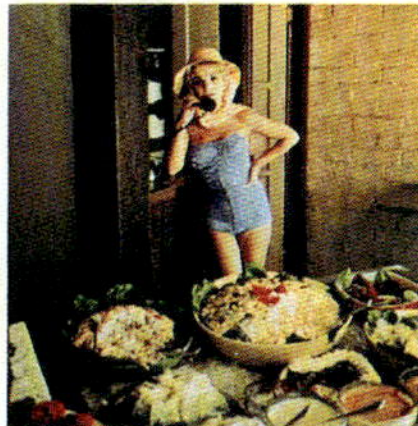

Mrs. Henry Dodge, of Beverly Hills, makes a pre-lunch call.

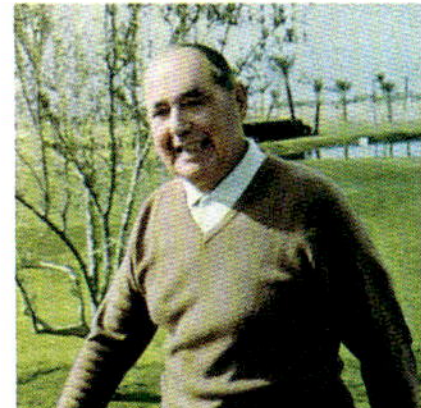

Eric Stainton, former vice president of National Distillers, soaks up sun.

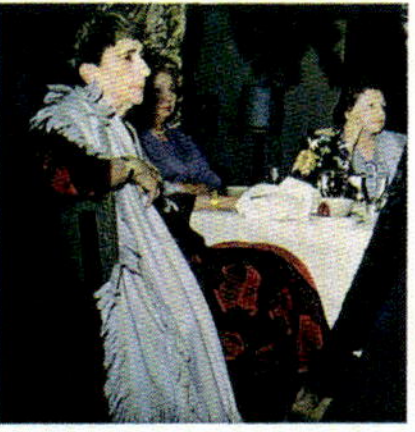

Mrs. Austin McManus, whose father was the first settler at Palm Springs.

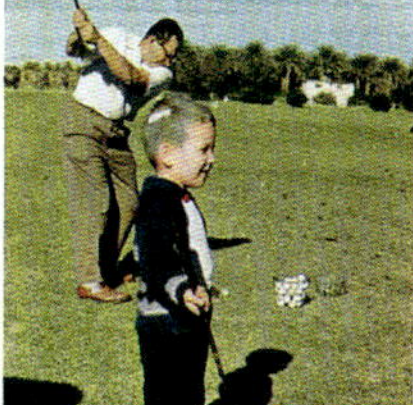

Local businessman Zachary Pitts and his son at Tamarisk Country Club.

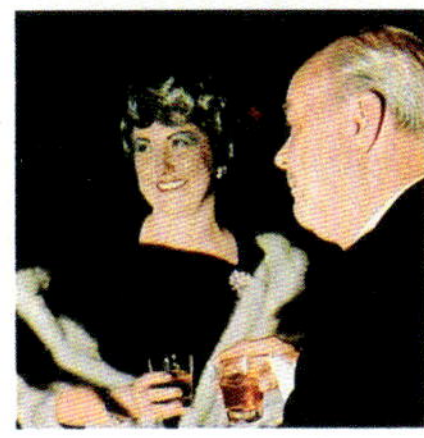

Mr. and Mrs. Lew Parrish of Los Angeles. He is a Teamsters' Union official.

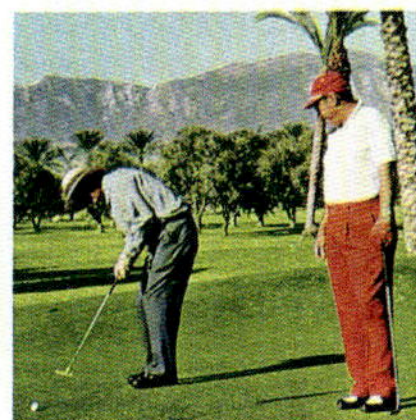

Richard Guelich of Buffalo, and Frank Godchaux of Louisiana.

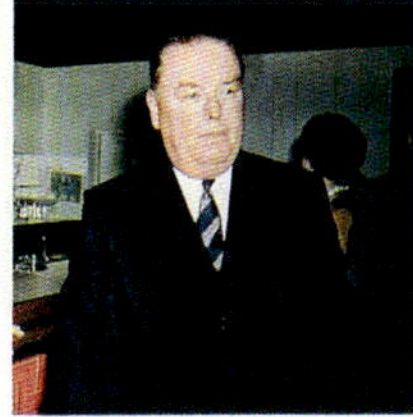

William Keck Jr., president of Superior Oil Co., at Eldorado Country Club.

Before President Eisenhower went to Palm Springs for the first of his golfing visits in 1954, that California desert town was only a regional resort. Overnight it became a winter resort with national drawing power. Now Dwight Eisenhower plans to spend a good deal of his time at Palm Springs. As fellow golfers here he will have such former government executives and businessmen as Marriner Eccles, Dan Kimball, "Dutch" Kindelberger, George Allen (who is also Eisenhower's neighbor in Gettysburg), Leonard Firestone, and Floyd Odlum.

Palm Springs, in the Coachella Valley, 105 miles east of Los Angeles, calls itself "the Winter Golf Capital of the World." There are twelve courses, one being built, and half a dozen on the drawing boards. The season begins in October with a flood of visitors that increases the population from an indigenous 15,000 to almost 50,000 on peak weekends. The crowd is mixed: the affluent of Wall Street, of Hollywood, and retired executives from the Midwest. By the end of May the visitors are gone.

Palm Springs grew slowly. In the 1920's it attracted actors and actresses from Hollywood who sought a refuge from Los Angeles' winter rains. Gradually business and professional men infiltrated the area. Soon raw desert that had been purchased for $100 an acre was selling for $50,000. Says one real-estate dealer of the future, "You can't lie fast enough to keep up with the truth."

Photographs by Robert Doisneau • RAPHO-GUILLUMETTE

Letters to Maurice Baquet • Robert Doisneau

Robert Doisneau's letters written in Palm Springs and addressed to his friend Maurice Baquet, who at the time was performing in a Broadway show.

Palm Springs
Riviera Hotel

Wednesday

My dear Maurice,

I am beginning to understand what soft colors are and, yet, I thought I knew them thanks to Ray Sugar's[1] automobile or the window displays of suburban hairdressers.

But since my arrival in Palm Springs it is delightful, especially in the evening—verdigris façades, orange-colored rooftops, and lilac-colored palm trees, there are other combinations of course, but they are all entrancing, incidentally everyone is very happy.

I feel as if I belong to another age, like a Louis XV armchair in an airfield or a cello in front of the Life building. That's a picture to make, and also a façade in the evening with your silhouette through a window and other silhouettes of people telephoning and bustling around in all the other lighted bay windows. Regarding telephones, a businessman's office with three telephones, the Statue of Liberty, the cinema street, a terrace with New York lit up.

For now, I am starting to meet millionaires, and there are a lot of them. I have a small white electric vehicle for driving around the greens and tomorrow a helicopter, to get a general idea.

I have been introduced to the millionaire golf-players as Robert-from-Paris. "A o are iou Hoariou," as they all say looking so pleased to meet me that it was flattering both for the profession and for Montrouge (Seine), and it is only the beginning, there are nineteen golf courses here, I will have contacts in oil, cinema, and the automobile industry.

I shall see you soon Maurice, I keep Charles[2] informed of my schedule, and, as he believes that idleness is the root of all evil, I have to be busy.

Regards from your photographer,

Robert-from-Paris

1 Sugar Ray Robinson, a world champion boxer.
2 Charles Rado, founder of the Rapho agency, who lived in New York.

Wednesday, November 30, 1960

My dear Maurice,

It is my last day in Palm Springs, tomorrow I am leaving for Hollywood, you mustn't tell Charles, but I am going to try and deal with Jerry Lewis quickly. I am quite impatient to see you because you can understand I am a bit knocked out, or rather, you cannot imagine the houses: swimming pools in the lounge for two elderly people, plastic gardens, fake Utrillo in the lavatories, spurting bottles on the bar and purple, green, mauve, I can't remember it all, rugs that I twist my ankles on, enough luxury for the Montrouge guys, I am the exotic one I realize. Nineteen golf courses, I have taken enough helicopter rides to make Lamorisse[3] sick, and pools, pools with nobody ever in them, and rich ladies and gentlemen, people talk figures to me with huge amounts of zeros just like the light-years in astronomy. I have no bearings but it must be said that everyone receives me with a simplicity and cheerfulness that the refined people of Lyon ignore, on top of all this an amazing and ceaselessly blue sky. Yesterday I was with the cowboys, there were real ones and fake ones, the real ones sang, it was wonderful, I was close to singing myself but pulled myself together just in time. I took a heap of pictures, who knows what they are worth?

At the end of the evening, it is as if I have blurred vision, and this morning my tongue is white, feeling melancholy with their confiture they put on steak, it upsets the digestion.

My dear Maurice, I can't wait for a jet ride to New York it would give me so much pleasure, your photographer,

Robert

3 Albert Lamorisse, producer and director of the films *Ballon rouge* and *Voyage en ballon,* in which travel by balloon is essential to the plots.

BIOGRAPHY • Robert Doisneau

1912 Born in Gentilly (Val-de-Marne, France) on April 14.

1926–29 Student at École Estienne.
Obtains a degree in lithographic engraving.

1930 Designer of letters and on-the-job training in pharmaceutical photography at Ullmann studios.

1931 Cameraman for André Vigneau.

1932 Sale of his first photoreport to the daily newspaper *L'Excelsior*.

1934–39 Industrial photographer at the Renault factories in Billancourt.

1939 Fired for repeated tardiness.
Meets Charles Rado, creator of the Rapho agency.
Becomes a freelance illustrative photographer.

1942 Meets Maximilian Vox, for whom he works on many commissions.

1945 Beginning of his collaboration with Pierre Betz, editor of the review *Le Point*.
Meets Blaise Cendrars in Aix-en-Provence.

1946 Returns to the Rapho agency now directed by Raymond Grosset.
Photoreports for the weekly newspaper *Action*.

1947 Meets Jacques Prévert and Robert Giraud.
Kodak Prize.

1949–51 Contract with *Vogue* magazine.

1956 Niépce Prize.

1960 Trip to the United States: photoreports in New York, Hollywood, and Palm Springs.

1966 Trip to Canada: photoreport in Montreal, a few days in New York.

1967 Photoreport in the USSR: "50 Years of Soviet Creations."

1971 French tour of national museums with Jacques Dubois.

1973 François Porcile's film, *Le Paris de Robert Doisneau*.

1975 Invited guest of Rencontres d'Arles photography festival.

1981 François Porcile's film, *Poète et piéton*.
Trip to New York.

1983 National Grand Prize of Photography.

1984 Takes part in the DATAR photography delegation.

1986 Balzac Prize.

1990 *Contacts video* (CNP/La Sept/Riff Production).

1992 *Bonjour, monsieur Doisneau*, film directed by Sabine Azéma (Riff Production).

1993 *Doisneau des villes et Doisneau des champs*, film directed by Patrick Cazals (FR3 Limousin-Poitou-Charente).

1994 Dies in Paris on April 1.

Acknowledgments

This journey to Palm Springs wouldn't have been possible if, in 2007, Scott Thode, director of photography for *Fortune* magazine, hadn't recovered the originals of the 1960 report from the magazine archives.

Thank you to him for having entrusted Jean-François Leroy with handing them over to us after a preview screening for the Visa pour l'Image Festival in Perpignan.

It then became clear that we had to do a book.

Thank you to Jean-Yves Quierry for having once again put his ideas, his talent, and his huge kindness into the department of artistic direction for this project.

Thank you to Gaëlle Lassée for enabling this project to turn into a book, for having thought that Jean-Paul Dubois, that America sometimes worries, would agree to unscramble the story of this strange, sweet, pink tribe. Thank you—infinitely—to him for having done so with so much talent.

Thank you to Corinne Trovarelli, Kate Mascaro, and the whole team at Flammarion, and Alain and Daniel Regard for accompanying us with a constant enthusiasm, which for us is so valuable in helping us to continue exploring our father's archives.

Annette Doisneau
Francine Deroudille

Translated from the French by Anna Hiddleston
Design: Jean-Yves Quierry
Copyediting: Kate Clark
Typesetting: Anne Lou Bissières
Proofreading: Helen Woodhall
Color Separation: Les Artisans du Regard, Paris
Printed in Italy by Musumeci

Simultaneously published in French

English-language edition

87, quai Panhard et Levassor
75647 Paris Cedex 13

editions.flammarion.com

18 19 20 4 3 2

ISBN: 978-2-08-030129-1

Dépôt légal: 03/2010